A 761

TECHNOLOGY AND
ECONOMIC DEVELOPMENT

Technology and Economic Development

A *Scientific American* Book

Penguin Books

Penguin Books Ltd, Harmondsworth, Middlesex, England
Penguin Books Pty Ltd, Ringwood, Victoria, Australia

—

First published in book form by Alfred A. Knopf 1963
Published in Pelican Books 1965

—

Copyright © Scientific American Inc., 1963

—

Made and printed in Great Britain by
C. Nicholls & Company Ltd
Set in Monotype Baskerville

—

The thirteen chapters in this
book originally appeared as
articles in the September 1963 issue
of *Scientific American*

Contents

7

Contents

Contents

Introduction

The present postwar period has now lasted eighteen years, already almost as long as the previous one. During this time the two great powers of the twentieth-century industrial civilization have been preoccupied with the presence of each other in this world.

History has nonetheless run on long enough to take a new turn. Abruptly, the great powers have concluded an agreement to suspend the testing of nuclear weapons above ground. This is a modest enough achievement. It does not halt the arms race, nor does it settle any outstanding political issue. In signing the agreement, however, the great powers have had to acknowledge the presence of other powers – not only the numerous large and small, old and new nations that joined them in the test ban but, even more notably, the powers that abstained. At this moment of depolarization in world political tensions, it becomes possible to consider the underlying causes of contemporary international conflict. These are to be found, without doubt, in the power vacuum of the poverty-stricken regions of the world and in the gathering revolution against poverty. As any look at the sites where the great powers have confronted each other will show – Greece, Korea, Iraq, Laos, the Congo, Vietnam, Cuba – the causes and cure of war are to be sought in the causes and cure of poverty.

The revolution against poverty is, in full historical perspective, an extension and continuation of the two-hundred-year-old industrial revolution that has created the historical novelty of the rich nation in which the entire population shares in increasing material well-being. Most members of the human species still live outside the pale of industrial civilization. They live in pre-industrial agricultural civilization much as their forebears did and in the same

Malthusian equilibrium with want. Their poverty is being mobilized politically; the new nations of the poor hold a commanding majority in the Assembly of the United Nations. The political mobilization of poverty is further amplified by urbanization; more than forty of the sixty-five cities with populations of a million or more are in the poor countries. In village as well as city, revolution becomes everywhere more inevitable, as infants survive in increasing numbers to become adults with unsatisfied needs.

The cruellest cost of this next phase of the industrial revolution will be its human cost. No one doubts that the indigenous economies of the poor nations must generate most of the capital required for industrialization. In accord with the well-tried precedents of the past, the necessary savings can be withheld from their inadequate current consumption by coercion and deprivation of the individual. It is at this point that the rich nations might intervene to change the course of history: the surpluses of high technology can balance the deficits of the poor nations and minimize the cost to the living generations of the rich and poor alike.

This is the human vision that men have in mind today when they speak of 'economic development'. The authors of this book have collaborated in a careful, professional appraisal of the possibility. In the light of history, after weighing the demands of a rapidly increasing population against the supply of natural resources, out of a lively comprehension of the relation of high technology to economic processes, and after a sympathetic review of the plans of representative developing countries, they concur in the finding that rational and human courses lie open to mankind in the present culmination of the industrial revolution.

This book is the product of a venture in science journalism. Its chapters made up the content of a single-topic issue of *Scientific American*, published in September 1963. The venture not only proved to be well-timed but promises to be an enduring contribution to the literature of economic development. The editors of the magazine here record their indebtedness to their colleagues at Alfred A. Knopf for so expeditiously extending the circulation and the life of *Technology and Economic Development* in book form.

September 1963   THE EDITORS*

Technology and
Economic Development

ASA BRIGGS

Introducing the problem of how nations can attain a state of self-sustaining growth. This chapter outlines the history of development and of the division of nations into 'rich' and 'poor'.

A circumstance new to history stretches the tensions of contemporary world politics. This is the widespread awareness of the division of nations into two classes, 'developed' and 'underdeveloped' in the parlance of the day, or, in plainer words, rich and poor. The contour lines of international economic inequality are easily drawn. To the class of the rich belong the nations of north-western Europe and those elsewhere in the temperate zones that were settled and organized by people of the same stock: the United States, Canada, Australia, and New Zealand. One non-European nation – Japan – should also be counted in the group, and recently another European nation, the U.S.S.R., has joined it. These nations, constituting less than a third of the human population, produce and consume more than two thirds of the world's goods. Their output is increasing more rapidly than their population, and they boast rising incomes per head.

Income per head hardly serves as a full measure of the position of the nations of the poor. The overwhelming majority of their populations are occupied in subsistence agriculture and live almost entirely outside the monetary systems of their meagre economies. For what the economic indices are worth, they show that between the poorest 1,500 million people – the bottom half of the human population – and the average standard of living prevailing in the rich countries the disparity is on the order of one to ten. More significantly, the indices show that the disparity between the two classes of nations is widening.

Poverty is not, of course, a new condition in human affairs. Some of the poor nations were once world powers and were held to be rich as well as powerful. Yet even though they have been placed at a disadvantage in recent years by the unfavourable terms of their relations with the rich nations, the situation in which their peoples live is not much worse than before. The rich nation is the novelty, and the development that makes entire nations rich is itself the pivotal development of modern history. To understand the increasing economic inequality of nations one must look outside the boundaries of economic theory. In the search for the causes, antecedents, and 'preconditions' of development it is necessary to turn to history, and the historian has his choice of starting points.

In the summer of 1454, one year after the fall of Constantinople to the Ottoman Turks, Enea Sylvio Piccolomini (later Pope Pius II), who has been described as one of the best-informed men in Europe, wrote gloomily that he could not see 'anything good' in prospect. Christendom was weak and divided, and internal conflicts as well as external challenges foretold likely destruction. He did not add, as he might have done, that there had also been a downsweep in the medieval economy. This was not the language of the age. His modest humanist hope was that he would be proved entirely wrong and that posterity would call him a liar rather than a prophet.

Within less than fifty years Europeans had pushed out adventurously far beyond the confines of Europe around the coast of Africa, toward India and south-east Asia and across the Atlantic. An Indian historian has described everything that has happened between then and our own times as the 'Vasco da Gama epoch' in world history. The search for wealth outside Europe's boundaries preceded the full mobilization of wealth within. Long before our own times Adam Smith, writing on the eve of the great industrial changes that transformed both society and men's ways of thinking about it, declared that the discovery of America and of a passage to the East Indies via the Cape of Good Hope were the two most important events in the history of mankind.

Within less than one hundred years after 1454 the great movements of thought and feeling to which historians long ago attached the labels of 'Renaissance' and 'Reformation' had further extended and disturbed the horizons of many Europeans. It is just as easy for twentieth-century writers to place the beginnings of 'modern times' in fifteenth- and sixteenth-century breaks with tradition as it was for Adam Smith. Those breaks now figure, however, less as spectacular events than as phases of processes, 'preconditions' of what was to happen later. The invention of the steam engine or the French Revolution, the one carrying with it a universal technology, the other a universal ideology, may today look like even bigger breaks. It is part of the task of the historian to scrutinize old labels carefully, to qualify large-scale generalizations, and to expose contradictory tendencies. Much that seems 'modern' has origins more remote than the eighteenth century. Much that was old in the fifteenth and sixteenth centuries has survived on a massive scale.

The least modern element in the first predatory phases of discovery was that the underdeveloped countries of today then seemed to be the great centres of wealth: the 'gorgeous East' and the South American El Dorado. The seventeenth-century English writer Thomas Mun, exaggerating and oversimplifying, maintained that the world commerce of his day consisted in the exchange of the mineral wealth of the new Indies in the West for the luxuries and refinements of the old Indies in the East. Francis Bacon referred to South America as 'the money-breeder of Europe'.

Between the beginnings of the age of world commerce, when new resources and markets were opened up, and the great industrial changes of the eighteenth and nineteenth centuries, when new methods of production were introduced, the wealth of nations was determined in large part by the struggle for empire and power. That struggle, which led to the eclipse of Spain and Portugal, the rise of the Netherlands, and the protracted contest between England and France, was world-wide in scale. American independence was one aspect of it. Concurrently, within Europe, no less significant but less dramatic changes in economic life were under way, later to culminate in industrial revolutions and the post-industrial division of nations into developed and underdeveloped.

By the early eighteenth century there were present in parts of Europe many of those economic and social ingredients whose absence is taken today as a sign or a cause of 'backwardness'. Among them were transport and credit facilities, many deriving from international trade; supplies of relatively skilled labour, some of it employed in industries with scattered and potentially expanding markets; and – not least – well-advanced acquisitive attitudes, congenial to both enterprise and capital accumulation. R. H. Tawney is not the only historian of capitalism to go back for his basic evidence not to the age of industrialism but to the shifts of values in the three centuries that preceded it.

It was during the last of these centuries that the 'scientific revolution' created new climates of opinion. 'The stream of English scientific thought, issuing from the teaching of Francis Bacon and enlarged by the genius of Boyle and Newton,' T. S. Ashton has written, 'was one of the main tributaries of the industrial revolution.' The statement cannot be disputed, even though many of the first inventors who transformed ways of production were men of little science. Practical and empirical, they were more interested in solving an immediate problem than in speculating about nature. The technical ascendancy of science belongs to the nineteenth and twentieth centuries, not the eighteenth.

Britain was the centre of the first industrial revolution. Throughout the first decades of the nineteenth century more than half of the world's industrial output was concentrated in an island with only about two per cent of the world's population. The British industrial revolution, the first in a sequence, became a classic model, even if it was a misleading model. From it Karl Marx deduced that 'the industrially more developed country presents to the less developed country a picture of the latter's future'. The forecast, involving as it did both the premiss of economic growth and the threat of social conflict, contrasts sharply with Adam Smith's pre-industrial forecast of a 'stationary state', in which the existing methods of production would have been 'improved' as far as they could possibly be improved and economic growth would have ceased.

The 'causes' of the British industrial revolution, therefore, have more than local interest. Historians are still arguing about the weighting of the various factors that contributed to the upsurge of growth, particularly in the 1780s. What seems clear is that, in addition to the cumulative build-up of economic power on the high seas and overseas and the social development of a community that encouraged innovation and thrift, urgent challenges had to be overcome before there could be an immense spurt in invention, investment, production, and trade. The slowing down of a previous rate of agricultural expansion and the peculiar exigencies of unprecedented population growth may explain difficult questions relating to timing. There are also long-term technical questions, however, in relation to the exploitation of iron and the development of steam power. It has even been argued that Britain had to leap ahead if it was not to lumber back.

Businessmen of the time often gave simple answers. 'We want as many spotted Muslins and fancy Muslins as you can make', a Northern cotton spinner was informed by his London agents in 1786. 'You have many competitors, we hear, coming forward. . . . You must give a look to Invention. Industry you have in abundance. . . . We expect to hear from you as soon as possible, and as the Sun shines let us make the Hay.' There were no ways to increase output to meet rising demand without new processes and new forms of organization. As a knowledgeable Manchester man put it in 1783: 'No exertion of the manufacturers or workmen could have answered the demands of trade without the introduction of spinning jennies'.

Thus at the very time American independence was ratified Britain was finding new sources of economic strength. Between 1781 and 1800 the imports of raw cotton quintupled, pig iron production quadrupled, foreign trade (whether measured in shipping tonnage cleared from the ports or in export and import values) nearly tripled and total industrial production doubled.

A contemporary writer with a precocious statistical sense drew rhetorical conclusions. 'An era has arrived in the affairs of the British Empire', wrote Patrick Colquhoun in 1814, just before the last of the great wars between Britain and France came to an end, 'when resources have been discovered which have excited the wonder, the astonishment and perhaps the envy of the civilized world'. He moved from rhetoric to social generalization.

It is with nations as it is with individuals who are in train of acquiring property. At first, progress is slow until a certain amount is obtained, after which, as wealth has a creative power under skillful and judicious management, the accumulation becomes more and more rapid, increasing often beyond a geometrical ratio, expanding in all directions, diffusing its influence wherever talents and industry prevail, and thereby extending the resources by which riches are obtained by communicating the power of acquiring it to thousands who have remained without wealth in countries less opulent.

The term 'industrial revolution' seems to have been invented by a French economist, Jérôme Adolphe Blanqui, in 1827. Before this, however, James Watt and Richard Arkwright had already been compared to Mirabeau and Robespierre, and smoke to propaganda. Something more had happened than mere acceleration of existing economic trends. Man's position had changed in relation to nature. Poets and prophets were as fascinated by steam power as millowners and ironmasters. Erasmus Darwin, the grandfather of Charles, wrote in 1792:

> Soon shall thy arm, UNCONQUER'D STEAM, afar
> Drag the slow barge, or drive the rapid car;
> Or in wide-waving wings expanded bear
> The flying chariot through the fields of air.
> Fair crews triumphant, leaning from above
> Shall wave their fluttering kerchiefs as they move;
> Or warrior bands alarm the gaping crowd,
> And armies shrink beneath the shadowy cloud.

In the first flash of enthusiasm there was immense imaginative appeal in technical discovery, just as there had been in the discovery of America. It was the recognition that nature could be tamed and the environment controlled that distinguished the industrial revolutions of the eighteenth and nineteenth centuries from the only comparable revolution in human productivity, that of the neolithic world, when settled agriculture took the place of hunting and food-gathering and a new division of labour transformed social and cultural processes.

The extent of the change can be measured not only in statistics of material progress but also in nineteenth-century social comment from Jean Charles Sismondi and Claude Henri Saint-Simon to John Stuart Mill and Marx. Saint-Simon wanted to change the words of the *Marseillaise* from '*enfants de la patrie*' to '*enfants de l'industrie*'. Politics for him was 'the science of production'. In 1848, the year of revolution, Mill wrote:

> All the nations which we are accustomed to call civilized, increase gradually in production and in population; and there is no reason to doubt that not only these nations will for some time continue so to increase but that most of the other nations of the world, including some not yet founded, will successively enter upon the same career.

Only the word 'gradually' is misleading. Industrialism

was to establish itself in sharp bursts, and once established it was to develop unevenly through boom and slump. It was also to create new social conflicts. Later writers emphasized, as the elder Arnold Toynbee did in his pioneer study of the 1880s, *Lectures on the Industrial Revolution of the 18th Century in England*, the social consequence of steam power – its effects on men's relations not with nature but with one another.

Not only were owners of capital often pitted against owners of land – town versus country, competition versus monopoly, progress versus tradition were some of the battle cries – but also there was a new division between 'capital' and 'labour'. It was to this division that Marx turned his attention, maintaining that in the very processes of industrial expansion 'classes' were being formed that were inexorably antagonistic. The rich would become richer and the poor poorer. Unlike traditionalist writers who bemoaned the decay of an old social order, Marx welcomed the transformation and the social revolution he thought it would ultimately entail. The melancholy conservative reaction was well expressed by Henri Frédéric Amiel in 1851:

> The statistician will register a growing progress and the novelist a gradual decline. . . . The useful will take the place of the beautiful, industry of art, political economy of religion, and arithmetic of poetry.

These contrasting pictures of the future were painted at a time when Europe was still primarily an agricultural continent with no more than patches of industry. Even these patches were frequently to be found among forests and besides streams rather than in concentrated industrial areas. Marx and the early British socialists before him might talk of a 'working class', but in Europe craftsmen far outnumbered factory workers and even in Britain there were far more domestic servants than textile workers. When the Great Exhibition of 1851 was held in the specially built Crystal Palace to illustrate 'the progress of mankind', there was no doubt that Britain was a workshop of the world.

During the early stages of industrialization the two master commodities were coal and iron. They took the place of wood, wind, and water at the centre of the new technology. The two materials were associated both geographically and economically; their close geographical proximity often created 'black country'. Their economic interdependence was expressed most strikingly in the great symbol of early industrialization: the steam locomotive puffing its way over 'iron roads'. It is not surprising that contemporaries saw the building of railroads as the beginning of a new world. 'We who lived before railways', wrote William Makepeace Thackeray, 'and survive out of the ancient world, are like Father Noah and his family out of the Ark. The children will gather round and say to us patriarchs, "Tell us, grandpa, about the old world."'

Others saw railroads as sinews of the economy and vitalizing influences on society. Heinrich von Treitschke, the ideologue of German nationalism, believed that railways, 'dragged the German nation from its stagnation'. Count Sergei Yulievich Witte, the Russian engineer and exponent of industrialization, set out to make railroads the foundation of a new economy in Russia in the 1890s; economic historians have been unanimous in pointing to Russian railroad building as 'the fulcrum round which the industrial level of the country was being rapidly lifted' during that decade.

The identification of industrialization with 'carboniferous capitalism', which was simply one phase of industrialization, has had lasting results. Along with a waste of economic resources there was a marked deterioration in the human environment in the new industrial areas. At the very time when science was suggesting that 'fate' was really amenable to social control, a new framework of social necessity was being constructed. The mill chimney and the slag heap dominated the horizon and set the scene for the social conflicts that also came to be identified with capitalism – conflicts centring not only on wages but also on status and authority, the length of the working day and the right to security.

Whatever the technology that activates industrial revolutions, the disturbance of old traditions and institutions and the imposition of unfamiliar rhythms of work and leisure are bound to bring social upheavals. But the coal-and-iron technology of the first industrial revolutions accentuated all the human difficulties. It is not surprising that in nineteenth-century Britain aesthetic and social protest converged in the writings of John Ruskin and William Morris. The same tradition of protest continued to exert a powerful influence, however, even after iron had given way to steel as a master material and electricity had provided a new source of power.

In this next age of technology Britain pioneered new schemes of social welfare but failed to hold its own economically. It was not only that other nations possessed greater physical resources which they could develop at lower cost; there was also a withering of enterprise in Britain. The rate of expansion slowed and British industry failed to participate fully in the new developments in steel – even though some of the basic inventions were British – in machine tools, electrical engineering, and chemicals.

Germany and the United States were the countries that took the lead in these industries of the future. By 1886 the United States had replaced Britain as the world's largest steel producer; Germany too was ahead by 1900. In machine tools the United States set a new pattern of standardization, the precondition of mass production. In the building of its electrical and chemical industries Germany, with the most advanced European system of scientific and technological education, became a 'new model' of industrialization. Output of sulphuric acid and alkalis rose eight times between 1870 and 1900; that of dyestuffs, in which Germany held a near monopoly, rose four times during the same period.

In both the United States and Germany the big industrial concern came to dominate manufacturing industry. The resulting concentration of economic power contrasted sharply with the diffusion of economic power during the early stages of the British industrial revolution. There was talk in the United States of 'titans' and in Germany of 'industrial Bismarcks'. Many of the great corporations of the twentieth century had their origins in the last decade of the nineteenth.

This was not the only difference between the British industrial revolution and the industrial revolutions that followed. In Britain little reliance had been placed on the state; everything had depended on a partnership of inventors and businessmen. The theory of the revolution – if there was a theory – was self-help in the industrial sphere and free trade between nations. In Germany the power of the state was harnessed to assist industrialization. In the United States the emerging industrial power enlisted the benevolent patronage of the Federal and state governments in the allocation of the continent's rich resources and the maintenance of a social and political climate congenial to its growth.

There was a traditional sanction for the German reliance on the state, but it was given eloquent new expression in the late nineteenth century. As Gustav Schmoller, an influential professor of economics, put it in 1884:

It was clearly those governments which understood best how to place the might of their fleets and the apparatus of their customs and navigation laws at the service of the economic interests of the nation with speed, boldness and clear purpose which thereby obtained the lead in the struggle and the riches of industrial prosperity.

At the same time the riches of prosperity added to the power of the state. The newly unified German state grew stronger as the industrial economy grew stronger. Dependence on tariffs, the direct intervention by bankers in the structure and control of industry, and the encouragement by the courts and the government of cartels and large-scale industrial organizations were all parts of the pattern.

The idea of using political power to hasten industrialization has become a commonplace in the twentieth century. Protests against industrialism have been less vociferous than demands for more industrialization. Not only has nationalism come to be closely associated with industrial strength and economic independence, but socialism also, which began with industrial discontent, has dwelt increasingly on economic 'planning'. Whereas in nineteenth-century Britain transfers of political power followed industrialization as railroads followed factories and furnaces, in many twentieth-century countries the existence of a 'progressive' and 'dynamic' directing political power has come to be considered a precondition to industrialization, much as Witte held railroads to be. Economic and social historians have spoken increasingly of innovating élites instead of entrepreneurs, the protagonists of classical economics. The more backward the economy, they argue, the more directly the state has had to intervene in the encouragement of industrialization, the greater has been the pressure for large-scale plant and the most up-to-date technology, and the more necessary has it been to proclaim a gospel of industrialism. In the 'neo-classic' industrial revolutions the incentive to 'get rich quick' has seldom proved a sufficient motive; 'development' has had to be advocated in more general terms.

Even before 1914, when industrialization was widening the income gap between the countries now classified as 'developed' and 'underdeveloped', Japan had joined Germany and the United States as a new centre of industrial revolution. In Japan, as in Germany, economic and political processes ran together in close harness. As a result of political and social revolutions in the 1860s Japan was able to break with enough of its tradition to carry out a deliberate industrial revolution. Samurai bureaucrats embarked on a sweeping 'westernization', although they took care not to destroy existing social structures. The state itself initiated strategic enterprises, facilitated the borrowing of advanced technology from abroad, and pursued a fiscal policy that encouraged the businessman and fixed the burden of forced savings on the farmer.

Between 1907 and 1914 Japan achieved an annual growth rate of more than eight per cent. 'By 1914', wrote William W. Lockwood, the historian of Japan's spectacular development, 'Japanese industrial capitalism was still weak and rudimentary by comparison with the advanced economies of the West. But it had now emerged from its formative stage.' During and after the First World War it was to profit from its industrial lead in Asia as Britain had profited from its lead in Europe one hundred and fifty years before. It was also to be in the vanguard of the third revolution of industrial technology based on plastics, new metals, and electronics.

Russia, which also increased its industrial output by eight per cent a year during its great forward leap of the 1890s, relied on somewhat similar devices, notably fiscal pressure on the peasants and the acquisition of technology from abroad. After the revolution of 1917 and the economic vicissitudes leading up to the promulgation of the first and second Five Year Plans, there evolved a militant ideology of industrialization. In the eighteenth century Britain and France had offered different, if complementary, revolutions to the world; the first was economic, the second political. The U.S.S.R. sought to offer both in one package. The ideology of industrial change would appeal to 'poor nations', it was felt, at least as strongly as socialist ideology had appealed to poor individuals or classes in the stormy years of iron and coal industrialization. Speed and scale were both emphasized. So too was sacrifice – the deliberate concentration on heavy industry and capital investment and the forcible limitation of consumption.

This model, reinforced as it has been with the factual evidence of an exceptionally high growth rate, has probably had more appeal than the ideology of communism itself. The appeal has influenced quite different kinds of society, although the universal applicability of the model is just

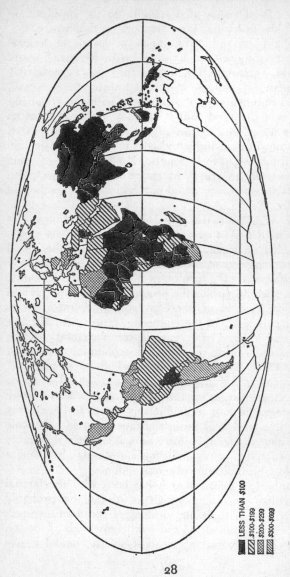

LESS THAN $100
$100–$199
$200–$299
$300–$699

UNDERDEVELOPED COUNTRIES are grouped here according to their average per capita incomes for 1957–9, based on available U.N. statistics and some estimates. Income, commonly accepted as a rough gauge of development, does not tell the whole story: Japan, for example, is considered developed although its per capita income is not high.

as much open to question as the universal applicability of the British model was open to question in the nineteenth century. More recently economists have directed increasing attention to the place in economic growth not of heavy industry but of agriculture. They have also stressed the subtleties of development. Industrial revolutions require more than political enthusiasm. 'Economic development is a process', John K. Galbraith, then U.S. Ambassador to India, told an Indian audience in 1961, 'that extends in range from new nations of Africa only slightly removed from their tribal structure to the elaborate economic and social apparatus of Western nations. At each stage along this continuum there is an appropriate policy for further advance. What is appropriate at one stage is wrong at another.'

In the changing context of argument and action the industrial experience of the richest industrial country in the world – the United States – has general relevance. Industrialization in the United States proceeded in a number of clearly defined spurts: the first between 1837, a year of depression, and the Civil War; the second in the decade and a half following the end of the war; and the third in the 1890s. Although there was a marked trend in each of these three periods to increase the relative share in production of producers' goods, equipment, and machines, emphasis in the twentieth century has been increasingly placed on the great expansion of consumers' goods. The United States, with its huge domestic market, has used the new technology to transform not only the standard of life of all its inhabitants but also their whole pattern of daily living. The consumer was deliberately placed at the centre of the industrial complex. The resulting dazzle of affluence contrasts sharply with the grim facts of poverty in underdeveloped countries and with the compelling 'puritan' philosophy of sacrifice based on investment for investment's sake.

Beyond doubt the problems centring on development and

underdevelopment furnish the principal preoccupation of contemporary political, economic, and social theory. Before the First World War it was taken for granted that there was a natural division in the world between manufacturing countries and primary producing countries – the black and the green. This assumption did not suppose either that relative power within the group of manufacturing countries was fixed for all time or that the gap between the rich countries and the poor countries was destined to go on widening forever. Yet it did close minds to a number of problems that are now felt to be fascinating as well as important.

Within the developed countries the facts of inequality between societies have lately begun to shock. The body of world statistics, gathered for the first time by the technical agencies of the League of Nations and now powerfully amplified by the international civil service of the United Nations, has exposed not only inequality but also the ugly mechanism of the 'Malthusian trap' in which two thirds of mankind is imprisoned. Kingsley Davis shows in his chapter on population, how the twenty or so developed nations have made their escape and prays that increase in the rate of production may exceed the rate of population growth elsewhere and make it possible for other nations to follow. As for food, water, energy, and minerals, the authors of other chapters find that supply is a function of the dynamic international variable, technology.

Yet although technology is international, political facts and attitudes remain stubbornly national. The spell of nationalism is strongest in the ex-colonies of 'developed' nations with empires. Political independence, it is felt, must be ratified by economic liberation. Any economic gains colonies may have secured through their place in the decaying empires are brushed aside, and the complicity of the rich in the poverty of the poor nations supplies the negative mould that shapes the plans of development. It is the 'distortions' of colonialism that count, not its untapping of world resources. As Wassily Leontief shows in 'The Structure of Development', page 129, the under-developed economies often present a 'mirror image' of the developed. Nigeria, for example, exports a few 'single crop' products of plantation agriculture and imports the diversity of goods produced by the advanced industrial economies. Other underdeveloped countries are engaged in shipping out their 'lifeblood' in the form of irreplaceable mineral resources. Each of these countries in turn, ex-colony or not, now seeks to import the technology necessary to the building of an indigenous, diversified, self-sustaining industrial economy.

Yet in spite of all the brave planning and even the beginnings of industrialization in countries such as India, the inequalities between nations are increasing. More than ninety per cent of the world's industrial output is still concentrated in areas inhabited by people of European origin. Even if underdeveloped countries were to increase their average incomes ten times faster than the economically advanced countries, the gap would still be wide. Given both population pressure and political pressure, is it possible to live peaceably in a world where such inequalities are being aggravated rather than attenuated and where dreams of development are sometimes frustrated?

Development is intimately bound up with twentieth-century shifts in power and conflicts of power, with mainland China, as well as the U.S.S.R., now taking the stage. The dynamic forces of industrialization are as much an element in contemporary international politics as the quest for gold and spices was in the era of mercantile expansion. The countries of the temperate zones once turned to the tropics for riches. Now the tropics – Brazil, for example, whose gold found its way through Portugal and Spain to finance the industrial revolution of Britain – turn to the temperate countries for know-how that cannot be transported in ships or by formula.

Whether, as Abba Eban of Israel has proposed, the 'new

nations do not have to tread long and tormented paths ...
and can skip the turbulent phases through which Western
industrial revolutions had to pass', depends in decisive
part on the politics and social disposition of the developed
nations. As Edward S. Mason shows in 'The Planning of
Development', page 209, the West is called on not only for
'aid' but also for tolerance of the new modes in which the
developing nations will assert their liberation from poverty.
Attitudes deriving from inequality can help or hinder such
tolerance. Consciences can be stirred, but there are also
built-in feelings of 'inferiority' and 'superiority'. In balance, a twentieth-century Piccolomini might see some good
in prospect, provided, that is, that we have imaginations
powerful enough to bridge the gulf between the different
worlds of our own making.

Population

KINGSLEY DAVIS

At the current growth rate the world's population would multiply sixfold in a century. Recent history suggests, however, that the rate will be cut by people acting in their own private interest.

Just as the nation-state is a modern phenomenon, so is the explosive increase of the human population. For hundreds of millenniums Homo sapiens was a sparsely distributed animal. As long as this held true, man could enjoy a low mortality in comparison to other species and could thus breed slowly in relation to his size. Under primitive conditions, however, crowding tended to raise the death rates from famine, disease, and warfare. Yet man's fellow mammals even then might well have voted him the animal most likely to succeed. He had certain traits that portended future dominance: a wide global dispersion, a tolerance for a large variety of foods (assisted by his early adoption of cooking), and a reliance on group cooperation and socially transmitted techniques. It was only a matter of time before he and his kind would learn how to live together in communities without paying the penalty of high death rates.

Man remained sparsely distributed during the neolithic revolution, in spite of such advances as the domestication of plants and animals and the invention of textiles and pottery. Epidemics and pillage still held him back, and new kinds of man-made disasters arose from erosion, flooding, and crop failure. Indeed, the rate of growth of the world population remained low right up to the sixteenth and seventeenth centuries.

Then came a spectacular quickening of the earth's human increase. Between 1650 and 1850 the annual rate of increase doubled, and by the 1920s it had doubled again.

After World War II, in the decade from 1950 to 1960, it took another big jump. The human population is now growing at a rate that is impossible to sustain for more than a moment of geologic time.

Since 1940 the world population has grown from about 2,500 million to 3,200 million. This increase, within twenty-three years, is more than the *total* estimated population of the earth in 1800. If the human population were to continue to grow at the rate of the past decade, within one hundred years it would be multiplied sixfold.

Projections indicate that in the next four decades the growth will be even more rapid. The United Nations' 'medium' projections give a rate during the closing decades of this century high enough, if continued, to multiply the world population sevenfold in one hundred years. These projections are based on the assumption that the changes in mortality and fertility in regions in various stages of development will be roughly like those of the recent past. They do not, of course, forecast the actual population, which may turn out to be a thousand million or two greater than that projected for the year 2000 or to be virtually nil. So far the U.N. projections, like most others in recent decades, are proving conservative. In 1960 the world population was 75 million greater than the figure given by the U.N.'s 'high' projection (published in 1958 and based on data up to 1955).

In order to understand why the revolutionary rise of world population has occurred, we cannot confine ourselves to the global trend, because this trend is a summation of what is happening in regions that are at any one time quite different with respect to their stage of development. For instance, the first step in the demographic evolution of modern nations – a decline in the death rate – began in north-western Europe long before it started elsewhere. As a result, although population growth is now slower in this area than in the rest of the world, it was here that the unprecedented upsurge in human numbers began. Being most advanced in demographic development, north-western Europe is a good place to start in our analysis of modern population dynamics.

In the late medieval period the average life expectancy in England, according to life tables compiled by the historian J. C. Russell, was about twenty-seven years. At the end of the seventeenth century and during most of the eighteenth it was about thirty-one in England, France, and Sweden, and in the first half of the nineteenth century it advanced to forty-one.

The old but reliable vital statistics from Denmark, Norway, and Sweden show that the death rate declined erratically up to 1790, then steadily and more rapidly. Meanwhile the birth rate remained remarkably stable (until the latter part of the nineteenth century). The result was a marked increase in the excess of births over deaths, or what demographers call natural increase. In the century from about 1815 until World War I the average annual increase in the three Scandinavian countries was 11.8 per 1,000 – nearly five times what it had been in the middle of the eighteenth century, and sufficient to triple the population in one hundred years.

For a long time the population of north-western Europe showed little reaction to this rapid natural increase. But when it came, the reaction was emphatic; a wide variety of responses occurred, all of which tended to reduce the growth of the population. For example, in the latter part of the nineteenth century people began to emigrate from Europe by the millions, mainly to America, Australia, and South Africa. Between 1846 and 1932 an estimated 27 million people emigrated overseas from Europe's ten most advanced countries. The three Scandinavian countries alone sent out 2.4 million, so that in 1915 their combined population was 11.1 million instead of the 14.2 million it would otherwise have been.

In addition to this unprecedented exodus, there were other responses, all of which tended to reduce the birth rate. In spite of opposition from church and state, agitation for birth control began and induced abortions became common. The age at marriage rose. Childlessness became frequent. The result was a decline in the birth rate that eventually overtook the continuing decline in the death rate. By the 1930s most of the industrial European countries had age-specific fertility rates so low that, if the rates had continued at that level, the population would eventually have ceased to replace itself.

In explaining this vigorous reaction one gets little help from two popular clichés. One of these – that population growth is good for business – would hardly explain why Europeans were so bent on stopping population growth. The other – that numerical limitation comes from the threat of poverty because 'population always presses on the means of subsistence' – is factually untrue. In every one of the industrializing countries of Europe economic growth outpaced population growth. In the United Kingdom, for example, the real per capita income increased 2.3 times between the periods 1855–9 and 1910–14. In Denmark from 1770 to 1914 the rise of the net domestic product in constant prices was 2.5 times the natural increase rate; in Norway and Sweden from the 1860s to 1914 it was respectively 1.4 and 2.7 times the natural increase rate. Clearly the strenuous efforts to lessen population growth were due to some stimulus other than poverty.

The stimulus, in my view, arose from the clash between new opportunities on the one hand and larger families on the other. The modernizing society of north-western Europe necessarily offered new opportunities to people of all classes: new ways of gaining wealth, new means of rising socially, new symbols of status. In order to take advantage of those opportunities, however, the individual and his children required education, special skills, capital, and mobility – none of which was facilitated by an improvident marriage or a large family. Yet because mortality was being reduced (and reduced more successfully in the

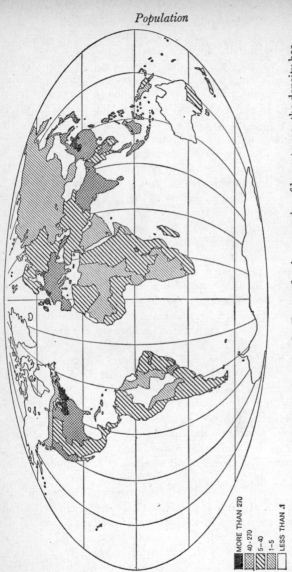

POPULATION MAP shows density as of 1961. Except for the countries of largest area, the density has been averaged within the boundaries of each nation. The densities are given in terms of the number of people per square kilometre. The data are primarily from U.N. publications.

MORE THAN 270
40 - 270
5 - 40
1 - 5
LESS THAN 1

childhood than in the adult ages) the size of families had become potentially larger than before. In Sweden, for instance, the mortality of the period 1755–75 allowed only 6.1 out of every 10 children born to reach the age of ten, whereas the mortality of 1901–10 allowed 8.5 to survive to that age. In order to avoid the threat of a large family to his own and his children's socio-economic position, the individual tended to postpone or avoid marriage and to limit reproduction within marriage by every means available. Urban residents had to contend particularly with the cost and inconvenience of young children in the city. Rural families had to adjust to the lack of enough land to provide for new marriages when the children reached marriageable age. Land had become less available not only because of the plethora of families with numerous youths but also because, with modernization, more capital was needed per farm and because the old folks, living longer, held on to the property. As a result farm youths postponed marriage, flocked to the cities, or went overseas.

In such terms we can account for the paradox that, as the progressive European nations became richer, their population growth slowed down. The process of economic development itself provided the motives for curtailment of reproduction, as the British sociologist J. A. Banks has made clear in his book *Prosperity and Parenthood*. We can see now that in all modern nations the long-run trend is one of low mortality, a relatively modest rate of reproduction, and slow population growth. This is an efficient demographic system that allows such countries, in spite of their 'maturity', to continue to advance economically at an impressive speed.

Naturally the countries of north-western Europe did not all follow an identical pattern. Their stages differed somewhat in timing and in the pattern of preference among the various means of population control. France, for example, never attained as high a natural increase as Britain or Scandinavia did. This was due not solely to an earlier decline in the birth rate, as is often assumed, but also to a slower decline in the death rate. If we historically substitute the Swedish death rate for the French, we revise the natural increase upward by almost the same amount as we do by substituting the Swedish birth rate. In accounting for the early and easy drop in French fertility one recalls that France, already crowded in the eighteenth century and in the van of intellectual radicalism and sophistication, was likely to have a low threshold for the adoption of abortion and contraception. The death rate, however, remained comparatively high because France did not keep economic pace with her more rapidly industrializing neighbours. As a result the relatively small gap between births and deaths gave France a slower growth in population and a lesser rate of emigration.

Ireland also has its own demographic history, but like France it differs from the other countries in emphasis rather than in kind. The emphasis in Ireland's escape from human inflation was on emigration, late marriage, and permanent celibacy. By 1891 the median age at which Irish girls married was twenty-eight (compared with twenty-two in the United States at that date); nearly a fourth of the Irish women did not marry at all, and approximately a third of all Irish-born people lived outside of Ireland. These adjustments, begun with the famine of the 1840s and continuing with slight modifications until today, were so drastic that they made Ireland the only modern nation to experience an absolute decline in population. The total of 8.2 million in 1841 was reduced by 1901 to 4.5 million.

The Irish preferences among the means of population limitation seem to come from the island's position as a rural region participating only indirectly in the industrial revolution. For most of the Irish, land remained the basis for respectable matrimony. As land became inaccessible to young people they postponed marriage. In doing so they were not discouraged by their parents, who wished to keep control of the land, or by their religion. Their Catholicism,

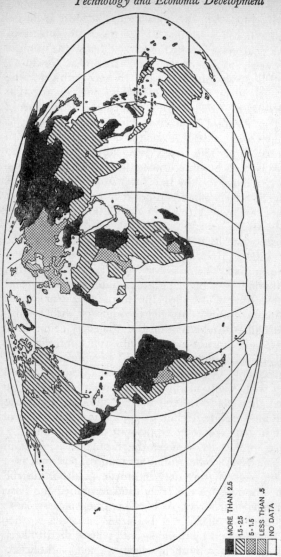

POPULATION MAP shows per cent increase per year between 1958 and 1961. Except for the countries of largest area the density has been averaged within the boundaries of each nation. The densities are given in terms of the number of people per square kilometre. The data are primarily from U.N. publications.

MORE THAN 2.5
1.5 - 2.5
.5 - 1.5
LESS THAN .5
NO DATA

which they embraced with exceptional vigour both because they were rural and because it was a rallying point for Irish nationalism as against the Protestant English, placed a high value on celibacy. The clergy, furthermore, were powerful enough to exercise strict control over courtship and thus to curtail illicit pregnancy and romance as factors leading to marriage. They were also able to exercise exceptional restraint on abortion and contraception. Although birth control was practised to some extent, as evidenced by a decline of fertility within marriage, its influence was so small as to make early marriage synonymous with a large family and therefore to be avoided. Marriage was also discouraged by the ban on divorce and by the lowest participation of married women in the labour force to be found in Europe. The country's failure to industrialize meant that the normal exodus from farms to cities was at the same time an exodus from Ireland itself.

Ireland and France illustrate contrasting variations on a common theme. Throughout north-western Europe the population upsurge resulting from the fall in death rates brought about a multiphasic reaction that eventually reduced the population growth to a modest pace. The main force behind this response was not poverty or hunger but the desire of the people involved to preserve or improve their social standing by grasping the opportunities offered by the newly emerging industrial society.

Is this an interpretation applicable to the history of any industrialized country, regardless of traditional culture? According to the evidence the answer is yes. We might expect it to be true, as it currently is, of the countries of southern and eastern Europe that are finally industrializing. The crucial test is offered by the only nation outside the European tradition to become industrialized: Japan. How closely does Japan's demographic evolution parallel that of north-western Europe?

If we superpose Japan's vital-rate curves on those of Scandinavia half a century earlier, we see a basically similar, although more rapid, development. The reported statistics, questionable up to 1920 but good after that, show a rapidly declining death rate as industrialization took hold after World War I. The rate of natural increase during the period from 1900 to 1940 was almost exactly the same as Scandinavia's between 1850 and 1920, averaging 12.1 per 1,000 population per year compared with Scandinavia's 12.3. And Japan's birth rate, like Europe's, began to dip until it was falling faster than the death rate, as it did in Europe. After the usual baby boom following World War II the decline in births was precipitous, amounting to fifty per cent from 1948 to 1960 – perhaps the swiftest drop in reproduction that has ever occurred in an entire nation. The rates of childbearing for women of various ages are so low that, if they continued indefinitely, they would not enable the Japanese population to replace itself.

In thus slowing their population growth have the Japanese used the same means as the peoples of north-western Europe did? Again, yes. Taboo-ridden Westerners have given disproportionate attention to two features of the change – the active role played by the Japanese government and the widespread resort to abortion – but neither of these disproves the similarity. It is true that since the war the Japanese government has pursued a birth-control policy more energetically than any government ever has before. It is also clear, however, that the Japanese people would have reduced their childbearing of their own accord. A marked decline in the reproduction rate had already set in by 1920, long before there was a government policy favouring this trend.

As for abortion, the Japanese are unusual only in admitting its extent. Less superstitious than Europeans about this subject, they keep reasonably good records of abortions, whereas most of the other countries have no accurate data. According to the Japanese records, registered abortions rose from 11.8 per 1,000 women of childbearing age in 1949 to a peak of 50.2 per 1,000 in 1955. We have no reliable historical information from Western countries, but we do know from many indirect indications that induced abortion played a tremendous role in the reduction of the birth rate in western Europe from 1900 to 1940 and that it still plays a considerable role. Furthermore, Christopher Tietze, of the National Committee for Maternal Health, has assembled records that show that in five eastern European countries where abortion has been legal for some time the rate has shot up recently in a manner strikingly similar to Japan's experience. In 1960–61 there were 139 abortions for every 100 births in Hungary, 58 per 100 births in Bulgaria, 54 in Czechoslovakia, and 34 in Poland. The countries of eastern Europe are in a developmental stage comparable to that of north-western Europe earlier in the century.

Abortion is by no means the sole factor in the decline of Japan's birth rate. Surveys made since 1950 show the use of contraception before that date, and increasing use thereafter. There is also a rising frequency of sterilization. Furthermore, as in Europe earlier, the Japanese are postponing marriage. The proportion of girls under twenty who have ever married fell from 17.7 per cent in 1920 to 1.8 per cent in 1955. In 1959 only about five per cent of the Japanese girls marrying for the first time were under twenty, whereas in the United States almost half of the new brides (48.5 per cent in the registration area) were that young.

Finally, Japan went through the same experience as western Europe in another respect – massive emigration. Up until World War II Japan sent millions of emigrants to various regions of Asia, Oceania, and the Americas.

In short, in response to a high rate of natural increase brought by declining mortality, Japan reacted in the same ways as the countries of north-western Europe did at a similar stage. Like the Europeans, the Japanese limited their population growth in their own private interest and that of their children in a developing society, rather than from any fear of absolute privation or any concern with overpopulation in their homeland. The nation's average 5.4 per cent annual growth in industrial output from 1913 to 1958 exceeded the performance of European countries at a similar stage.

As our final class of industrialized countries we must now consider the frontier group – the United States, Canada, Australia, New Zealand, South Africa, and Russia. These countries are distinguished from those of north-western Europe and Japan by their vast wealth of natural resources in relation to their populations; they are the genuinely affluent nations. They might be expected to show a demographic history somewhat different from that of Europe. In certain particulars they do, yet the general pattern is still much the same.

One of the differences is that the riches offered by their untapped resources invited immigration. All the frontier industrial countries except Russia received massive waves of emigrants from Europe. They therefore had a more rapid population growth than their industrializing predecessors had experienced. As frontier countries with great room for expansion, however, they were also characterized by considerable internal migration and continuing new opportunities. As a result their birth rates remained comparatively high. In the decade from 1950 to 1960, with continued immigration, these countries grew in population at an average rate of 2.13 per cent a year, compared with 1.76 per cent for the rest of the world. It was the four countries with the sparsest settlement (Canada, Australia, New Zealand, and South Africa), however, that accounted for this high rate; in the United States and the U.S.S.R. the growth rate was lower – 1.67 per cent a year.

Apparently, then, in pioneer industrial countries with an abundance of resources, population growth holds up at a higher level than in Japan or north-western Europe because the average individual feels it is easier for himself and his children to achieve a respectable place in the social scale. The immigrants attracted by the various opportunities normally begin at a low level and thus make the status of natives relatively better. People marry earlier and have slightly larger families. But this departure from the general pattern for industrial countries seems to be only temporary.

In the advanced frontier nations, as in north-western Europe, the birth rate began to fall sharply after 1880, and during the depression of the 1930s it was only about ten per cent higher than in Europe. Although the post-war baby boom has lasted longer than in other advanced countries, it is evidently starting to subside now, and the rate of immigration has diminished. There are factors at work in these affluent nations that will in all likelihood limit their population growth. They are among the most urbanized countries in the world, in spite of their low average population density. Their birth rates are extremely sensitive to business fluctuations and social changes. Furthermore, having in general the world's highest living standards, their demand for resources, already staggering, will become fantastic if both population and per capita consumption continue to rise rapidly, and their privileged position in the world may become less tolerated.

Let us shift now to the other side of the population picture: the non-industrial, or under-developed, countries.

As a class the non-industrial nations since 1930 have been growing in population about twice as fast as the industrial ones. This fact is so familiar and so taken for granted that its irony tends to escape us. When we think of it, it is astonishing that the world's most impoverished nations, many of them already overcrowded by any standard, should be generating additions to the population at the highest rate.

The underdeveloped countries have about sixty-nine per cent of the earth's adults – and some eighty per cent of the world's children. Hence the demographic situation itself tends to make the world constantly more under-developed, or impoverished, a fact that makes economic growth doubly difficult.

How can we account for the paradox that the world's poorest regions are producing the most people? One is tempted to believe that the underdeveloped countries are simply repeating history: that they are in the same phase of rapid growth the West experienced when it began to in-dustrialize and its death rates fell. If that is so, then sooner or later the developing areas will limit their population growth as the West did.

It is possible that this may prove to be true in the long run. But before we accept the comforting thought we should take a close look at the facts as they are.

In actuality the demography of the non-industrial countries today differs in essential respects from the early history of the present industrial nations. Most striking is the fact that their rate of human multiplication is far higher than the West's ever was. The peak of the industrial nations' natural increase rarely rose above 15 per 1,000 population per year; the highest rate in Scandinavia was 13, in England and Wales 14, and even in Japan it was slightly less than 15. True, the United States may have hit a figure of 30 per 1,000 in the early nineteenth century, but if so it was with the help of heavy immigration of young people (who swelled the births but not the deaths) and with the encouragement of an empty continent waiting for ex-ploitation.

In contrast, in the present underdeveloped but often crowded countries the natural increase per 1,000 population is everywhere extreme. In the decade from 1950 to 1960 it averaged 31.4 per year in Taiwan, 26.8 in Ceylon, 32.1 in Malaya, 26.7 in Mauritius, 27.7 in Albania, 31.8 in Mexico, 33.9 in El Salvador, and 37.3 in Costa Rica. These are not birth rates; they are the *excess* of births over deaths! At an annual natural increase of 30 per 1,000 a population will double itself in twenty-three years.

The population upsurge in the backward nations is apparently taking place at an earlier stage of development – or perhaps we should say *un*development – than it did in the now industrialized nations. In Britain, for instance, the peak of human multiplication came when the country was already highly industrialized and urbanized, with only a fifth of its working males in agriculture. Comparing four industrial countries at the peak of their natural increase in the nineteenth century (14.1 per 1,000 per year) with five non-industrial countries during their rapid growth in the 1950s (32.2 per 1,000 per year), I find that the industrial countries were 38.5 per cent urbanized and had 27.9 per cent of their labour force in manufacturing, whereas now the non-industrial countries are 29.4 per cent urbanized and have only 15.1 per cent of their people in manufacturing. In short, today's non-industrial populations are growing faster and at an earlier stage than was the case in the demographic cycle that accompanied industrialization in the nineteenth century.

As in the industrial nations, the main generator of the population upsurge in the underdeveloped countries has been a fall in the death rate. But their resulting excess of births over deaths has proceeded faster and farther, as a comparison of Ceylon in recent decades with Sweden in the 1800s shows.

In most of the underdeveloped nations the death rate has dropped with record speed. For example, the sugar-growing island of Mauritius in the Indian Ocean within an eight-year period after the war raised its average life expectancy from thirty-three to fifty-one – a gain that took Sweden one hundred and thirty years to achieve. Taiwan within two decades has increased its life expectancy from forty-three to sixty-three; it took the United States some eighty years to make this improvement for its white population. According to the records in eighteen underdeveloped countries, the crude death rate has dropped substantially in each decade since 1930; it fell some six

47

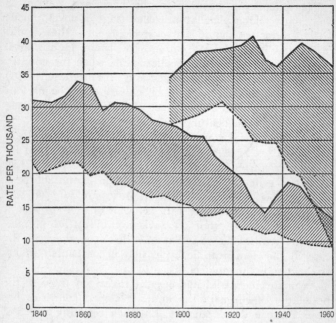

A NEW DEMOGRAPHIC PATTERN is appearing in the non-industrialized nations. The birth rate (*solid line*) has not been falling significantly, whereas the death rate (*broken line*) has dropped precipitously, as illustrated by Ceylon (*upper area*). The spread between the two rates has widened. In nations such as Sweden (*lower area*), however, the birth rate dropped during development long before the death rate was as low as in most underdeveloped countries today.

per cent in the 1930s and nearly 20 per cent in the 1950s, and according to the most recent available figures the decline in deaths is still accelerating.

The reasons for this sharp drop in mortality are in much dispute. There are two opposing theories. Many give the credit to modern medicine and public health measures. On the other hand, the public health spokesmen, rejecting the accusation of complicity in the world's population crisis, belittle their own role and maintain that the chief factor in the improvement of the death rate has been economic progress.

Those in the latter camp point out that the decline in the death rate in north-western Europe followed a steadily rising standard of living. Improvements in diet, clothing, housing, and working conditions raised the population's resistance to disease. As a result many dangerous ailments disappeared or subsided without specific medical attack. The same process, say the public health people, is now at work in the developing countries.

On the other side, most demographers and economists believe that economic conditions are no longer as important as they once were in strengthening a community's health. The development of medical science has provided lifesaving techniques and medicines that can be transported overnight to the most backward areas. A Stone Age people can be endowed with a low twentieth-century death rate within a few years, without waiting for the slow process of economic development or social change. International agencies and the governments of the affluent nations have been delighted to act as good Samaritans and send out public health missionaries to push disease-fighting programmes for the less developed countries.

The debate between the two views is hard to settle. Such evidence as we have indicates that there is truth on both sides. Certainly the newly evolving countries have made economic progress. Their economic advance, however, is not nearly rapid enough to account for the very swift decline in their death rates, nor do they show any clear correlation between economic growth and improvement in life expectancy. For example, in Mauritius during the five-year period from 1953 to 1958 the per capita income fell by 13 per cent, yet notwithstanding this there was a 36 per cent drop in the death rate. On the other hand, in the period between 1945 and 1960 Costa Rica had a 64 per cent increase in the per capita gross national product and a 55 per cent decline in the death rate. There seems to be no consistency – no significant correlation between the two trends when we look at the figures country by country. In fifteen underdeveloped countries for which such figures are available we find that the decline in death rate in the 1950s was strikingly uniform (about four per cent per year), although the nations varied greatly in economic progress – from no improvement to a 6 per cent annual growth in per capita income.

Our tentative conclusion must be, therefore, that the public health people are more efficient than they admit. The billions of dollars spent in public health work for under-developed areas has brought down death rates, irrespective of local economic conditions in these areas. The pro-grammes instituted by outsiders to control cholera, malaria, plague, and other diseases in these countries have succeeded. This does not mean that death control in underdeveloped countries has become wholly or permanent-ly independent of economic development, but that it has become temporarily so to an amazing degree.

Accordingly the unprecedented population growth in these countries bears little relation to their economic condition. The British economist Colin G. Clark has con-tended that rapid population growth stimulates economic progress. This idea acquires plausibility from the association between human increase and industrialization in the past and from the fact that in advanced countries today the birth rate (but not the death rate) tends to fluctuate with business conditions. In today's underdeveloped countries, however, there seems to be little or no visible connexion between economics and demography.

In these countries neither births nor deaths have been particularly responsive to economic change. Some of the highest rates of population growth ever known are occurring in areas that show no commensurate economic advance. In thirty-four such countries for which we have data, the correlation between population growth and economic gain during the 1950s was negligible, and the slight edge was on the negative side: −0.2. In twenty Latin-American countries during the period from 1954 to 1959, while the annual gain in per capita gross domestic product fell from an average of 2 per cent to 1.3 per cent, the population growth rate *rose* from 2.5 to 2.7 per cent per year.

All the evidence indicates that the population upsurge in the underdeveloped countries is not helping them to advance economically. On the contrary, it may well be interfering with their economic growth. A surplus of labour on the farms holds back the mechanization of agriculture. A rapid rise in the number of people to be maintained uses up income that might otherwise be utilized for long-term investment in education, equipment, and other capital needs. To put it in concrete terms, it is difficult to give a child the basic education he needs to become an engineer when he is one of eight children of an illiterate farmer who must support the family with the produce of two acres of ground.

By definition 'economic advance' means an increase in the amount of product per unit of human labour. This calls for investment in technology, in improvement of the skills of the labour force, and in administrative organization and planning. An economy that must spend a disproportionate share of its income in supporting the consumption needs of a growing population – and at a low level of consumption at that – finds growth difficult because it lacks capital for improvements.

A further complication lies in the process of urbanization. The shifts from villages and farmsteads to cities is seemingly an unavoidable and at best a painful part of economic development. It is most painful when the total population is skyrocketing; then the cities are bursting both from their own multiplication and from the stream of migrants from the villages. The latter do not move to cities because of the opportunities there. The opportunities are few and unemployment is prevalent. The migrants come, rather, because they are impelled by the lack of opportunity in the crowded rural areas. In the cities they hope to get something – a menial job, government relief, charities of the rich. I have recently estimated that if the population of India increases at the rate projected for it by the U.N., the net number of migrants to cities between 1960 and 2000 will be of the order of 99 to 201 million, and in 2000 the largest city will contain between 36 and 66 million inhabitants. One of the greatest problems now facing the governments of underdeveloped countries is what to do with these millions of penniless refugees from the excessively populated countryside.

Economic growth is not easy to achieve. So far, in spite of all the talk and the earnest efforts of underdeveloped nations, only one country outside the north-western European tradition has done so: Japan. The others are struggling with the handicap of a population growth greater than any industrializing country had to contend with in the past. A number of them now realize that this is a primary problem, and their governments are pursuing or contemplating large-scale programmes of birth limitation. They are receiving little help in this matter, however, from the industrial nations, which have so willingly helped them to lower their death rates.

The Christian nations withhold this help because of their official taboos against some of the means of birth limitation (although their own people privately use all these means). The Communist nations withhold it because limitation of population growth conflicts with official Marxist dogma (but Soviet citizens control births just as capitalist citizens do, and China is officially pursuing policies calculated to reduce the birth rate).

The West's preoccupation with the technology of contraception seems unjustified in view of its own history. The peoples of north-western Europe utilized all the available means of birth limitation once they had strong motives for such limitation. The main question, then, is whether or not the peoples of the present underdeveloped countries are likely to acquire such motivation in the near future. There are signs that they will. Surveys in India, Jamaica, and certain other areas give evidence of a growing desire among the people to reduce the size of their families. Furthermore, circumstances in the underdeveloped nations today are working more strongly in this direction than they did in north-western Europe in the nineteenth century.

As in that earlier day, poverty and deprivation alone are not likely to generate a slow-down of the birth rate. But personal aspirations are. The agrarian peoples of the backward countries now look to the industrialized, affluent fourth of the world. They nourish aspirations that come directly from New York, Paris, and Moscow. No more inclined to be satisfied with a bare subsistence than their wealthier fellows would be, they are demanding more goods, education, opportunity, and influence. And they are beginning to see that many of their desires are incompatible with the enlarged families that low mortality and customary reproduction are giving them.

They live amid a population density far greater than existed in nineteenth-century Europe. They have no place to which to emigrate, no beckoning continents to colonize. They have rich utopias to look at and industrial models to emulate, whereas the Europeans of the early 1800s did not know where they were going. The peoples of the underdeveloped, overpopulated countries therefore seem likely to start soon a multiphasic limitation of births such as began to sweep through Europe a century ago. Their governments appear ready to help them. Government policy in these countries is not quibbling over means or confining itself to birth-control technology; its primary task is to strengthen and accelerate the peoples' motivation for reproductive restraint.

Meanwhile the industrial countries also seem destined to apply brakes to their population growth. The steadily rising level of living, multiplied by the still growing numbers of people, is engendering a dizzying rate of consumption. It is beginning to produce painful scarcities of space, of clean water, of clean air, and of quietness. All of this may prompt more demographic moderation than these countries have already exercised.

Food

NEVIN S. SCRIMSHAW

The first task of a poor country is to improve both the quantity and the quality of its nutrition. Basically, this calls for education, not only in agriculture but also in food economics and technology.

Nearly half the world's population is underfed or otherwise malnourished. The lives of the people in the underdeveloped areas are dominated by the scramble for food to stay alive. Such people are perpetually tired, weak, and vulnerable to disease – prisoners of a vicious circle that keeps their productivity far below par and so defeats their efforts to feed their families adequately. Because their undernourishment begins soon after birth, it produces permanently depressing and irremediable effects on the population as a whole. Malnutrition and disease kill a high proportion of the children by the age of four; the death rates for these young children are 20 to 60 times higher than in the United States and western Europe. Among those who survive, few escape physical or mental retardation or both.

Obviously the first necessity, if the underdeveloped countries are to develop, is more and better food. Much has been said about the need for industrialization of these countries as the quickest and most effective way to raise their incomes and level of living. But they cannot industrialize successfully without a substantial improvement in their nourishment and human efficiency. This must depend primarily on improvement of their agriculture and utilization of food. In these countries from 60 to 80 per cent of the people are engaged in farming, but their productivity is so low that it falls far short of feeding the population. That stands as a roadblock against their advance. Unless they improve their food-producing efficiency, any diversion of

55

their working force to industry will only make their food problem more desperate.

Moreover, during the coming decades their food requirements will rise astronomically, both because of their rapid population growth and because of the demand for the better scale of living that comes with industrialization. The Food and Agriculture Organization of the United Nations has estimated that to provide a decent level of nutrition for the world's peoples the production of food will have to be doubled by 1980 and tripled by 2000.

Can the developing nations make the grade? Is our planet capable of feeding the hungry half of the world and supporting its vast, growing population? This is a complex question that involves many issues other than the volume of food production. Just as important are the conservation of food, the kinds of foods produced, and the ways in which food is used. Food supply is not merely a matter of the number of bushels of grain the farmer harvests or the number of chickens he raises. Other vital elements in the equation are the selection, handling, processing, storage, transportation, and marketing of the food crops. Each factor allows opportunities for improvement of efficiency that can greatly enhance the food supply.

Let us consider what science and technology have to contribute to the food problem.

The simplest way to increase food production, one might suppose, is to bring more land under cultivation and put more people to work on it. The U.S.S.R. and some of the underdeveloped countries have resorted to this straightforward approach, without notable success. It contains several fallacies. For one thing, it usually means moving into marginal land where the soil and climatic conditions give a poor return. Cultivation may quickly deplete this soil, ruining it for pasture or forest growth. It is often possible, of course, to turn such lands into useful farms by agricultural know-how; for instance, a sophisticated knowledge of how to use the available water through an irrigation system may reclaim semi-arid grasslands for crop-growing. But the cultivation of marginal lands is in any case unsuccessful unless it is carried out by farmers with a centuries-old tradition of experience or by modern experts with a detailed knowledge of the local conditions and the varieties of crops that are suitable for those conditions. Such knowledge is conspicuously absent in the under-developed countries.

Furthermore, we know that the highly developed countries have not increased the number of acres under cultivation but on the contrary have abandoned their marginal lands and steadily reduced the proportion of the population engaged in farming. Efficient farming calls for concentration on the most efficient lands, and it also results in greater production with fewer people. The United States, for example, produces a huge surplus of food with only about ten per cent of its people working on the farms.

The problem of the underdeveloped countries, then, is to increase the productivity of their farms and farmers. This would allow them to industrialize and to feed their people more adequately. It is not easy to accomplish, however. The peasant farmers are conservative and resistant to change in their methods of cultivation. The entire population needs to be indoctrinated in the possibilities offered by scientific agriculture, including the officials who must provide the necessary funds, planning, legislation, training, and research programmes. The underdeveloped countries are greatly in need of studies and experiments to help them to adapt modern agricultural methods to their own conditions.

During the past two decades some of these countries have increased their food production, but their populations have in the meantime grown faster; therefore they are farther behind than before. Furthermore, the food increase has been gained at the expense of using up marginal lands. In productivity per acre or per man they have not gained at all.

Meanwhile the efficiency of farming in the developed

countries has progressed phenomenally. In the United States the productivity per farm worker has tripled since 1940. With a 7 per cent reduction in the total acreage under cultivation, United States production of cereal grains has jumped 50 per cent; the increase in the corn output, thanks to hybrid corn, has been even greater.

The 'secret' of these improvements can be summed up in a few words: chemicals, mechanization, breeding, and feeding.

Fertilizers are an old story to farmers, even in backward countries, but the practitioners of modern farming have raised the use of chemical fertilizers to a high art. To these they have added a pharmacopoeia of chemicals for special purposes: poisons to kill insects, fungi, and other pests; plant-growth regulators to control weeds, force early sprouting, stimulate ripening, and prevent premature dropping of fruit; soil-conditioners to improve the physical characteristics of the soil. Most of these techniques and materials could easily be introduced on the farms of the underdeveloped areas. They require capital investment, but they would pay for themselves many times over in higher yields.

The mechanization of farming has become so familiar in Western countries that we have forgotten the many changes it has brought about. It has released for human food a great deal of land formerly devoted to growing feed for draught animals. Feeding fuel to a machine is cheaper than feeding a horse, and the machine needs less care and maintenance. The machine not only ploughs and cultivates but also digs ditches and postholes, loads and handles heavy materials, harvests, threshes, chops forage, cleans vegetables, and does many other things the intelligent horse could never do. It does all these things swiftly and virtually at a moment's notice, so that the farmer no longer has to worry about whether or not he can get a job done before threatening weather ruins his planting or his harvest.

The machine has also facilitated the building and

development of irrigation systems. It makes easy work of the construction of dams, the digging of water channels, and the pumping of water. In the United States irrigation has made it possible to increase the crop yield of Western lands by 50 to 100 per cent. In the arid zones of India and the Middle East, which for centuries have been entirely dependent on irrigation for their farming, extension of their systems with machinery would be a great boon. In some areas where enough water could be furnished by irrigation, two or three crops a year could be produced and the crops could be diversified.

Finally, a combination of selective breeding and efficient feeding has generated astonishing bounties in both plant and animal production. For most of the major plant crops, thanks to modern genetics, we have seen the development of new varieties that give a higher yield and are more resistant to disease. The same is true of the animals that supply our meat, milk, and eggs. 'Hybrid vigour' has become a magic phrase in the U.S. farm belt. Furthermore, the farmer today can buy selected seeds he knows will do certain specific things with high reliability: produce plants that mature faster, are adapted to a wide range of conditions, or grow to a uniform height, and all ripen at the same time so that they can be harvested by machine.

We now have wilt-resisting peas and cabbages, mosaic-resisting snap beans, virus-resisting potatoes, mildew-resisting cucumbers and lima beans, anthracnose-resisting watermelons, and leaf-spot-resisting strawberries. We have new cereal grains rich in high-quality protein, special squash rich in vitamin A, cottonseed from which the toxic pigment called gossypol has been bred out. We have cows that give richer milk, hogs that grow exceptionally fast on less feed, hogs with more lean meat and less fat, poultry with a high ratio of lean meat.

To improvement of the animal breeds the advanced countries have coupled scientific husbandry: finely calculated diets and rations, synthetic hormones, pesticides and sanitary stalls, drugs and vaccines to control disease, and many other measures that have heightened the efficiency of production. The results are most strikingly shown in poultry raising. There are now breeds of hens that lay more than two hundred eggs a year and broilers that grow to a three-pound market size within ten weeks. Diseases, waste motion, and costs have been sharply reduced. Raised in individual cages arrayed in batteries of hundreds or thousands, the chickens minimize the expenditure of energy by themselves and their caretakers and facilitate record-keeping, so that the less productive birds can easily be eliminated.

In general it would not be difficult to apply most of the agricultural improvements to the countries that need them so urgently. The main biological problem would be to select the right plants and animals for transfer to those countries. For instance, Temperate Zone varieties of corn and soybeans do not grow well in hotter areas; prize pigs from mild climates are often unable to nurse their young in the Tropics; plants and animals that are successful in one region may quickly succumb to diseases in another. But analysis of the ecological conditions and testing can resolve these problems. It is known, for example, that certain plants can readily be transplanted from areas in the United States to areas in Japan, because the climatic conditions are much the same. The identification and classification of such ecological analogues on a world-wide scale would greatly facilitate the transfer of agricultural techniques to the underdeveloped regions.

Aside from more efficient methods, however, those countries need a sounder over-all policy, which is to say, in most cases, more diversification of crops. Many of the underdeveloped nations are enslaved by a single cash crop, such as rubber, hemp, cotton, coffee, tea, sugar, or olive oil, with deadly effects on their basic food supply. It is true that the export of the single crop provides cash with which to buy food, but it places the country at the mercy of crop failure and price fluctuations in the world market. There have been periods when it has meant mass starvation for a whole region.

Without giving up its profitable crop, each country should be able to expand its own food production and achieve a better-balanced agricultural economy. In some cases it could improve its food supply immediately without radical changes. For example, the cotton-raising countries usually export the cottonseed-oil meal along with the fibre; instead they could keep the meal and use it for animal feed and even as human food.

Thus in their campaign against hunger the developing countries need first of all to increase their food production. The second way in which they could make great strides is by better food conservation or preservation. In this field the advanced countries have achieved improvements fully as spectacular as in production.

For food-raising Homo sapiens the perishability of foodstuffs has always been a major problem. Gradually he learned that his food supply would go further if he kept it edible longer by smoking, drying, or salting it, or by keeping it cool in caves, wells, snow, or ice from ponds. With limited effectiveness, these devices have served man for many centuries. But general food conservation on a large scale did not begin until the nineteenth century, with the arrival of the insulated refrigerator.

Within the past two decades we have seen freezing become a major means of preserving food in the United States. Still newer is the recent development of freeze-drying – a system of vacuum dehydration of frozen food that makes it possible to store many foods without refrigeration and still retain their fresh flavour and characteristic properties. This method is ideal for keeping food in tropical areas, but it is still comparatively expensive. Vacuum-drying without freezing, however, is less costly and can preserve certain foods with little change in their flavour or texture. Also cheaper than freeze-drying is the

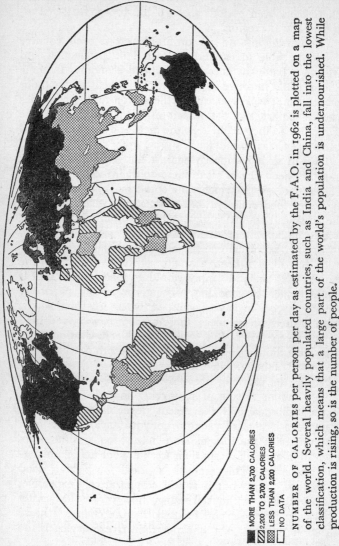

MORE THAN 2,700 CALORIES

2,200 TO 2,700 CALORIES

LESS THAN 2,200 CALORIES

NO DATA

NUMBER OF CALORIES per person per day as estimated by the F.A.O. in 1962 is plotted on a map of the world. Several heavily populated countries, such as India and China, fall into the lowest classification, which means that a large part of the world's population is undernourished. While production is rising, so is the number of people.

new process of foam-mat drying, which is particularly good for fruit juices and purées.

Sterilization of food by ionizing radiation, which once seemed very promising, now looks impractical, because it damages the flavour and nutritional value. But irradiation with smaller doses, in the pasteurization range, may help to prolong the storage life of foods, although they will have to be refrigerated. Bacon preserved by this process has recently been approved for sale in the United States. Another new technique is dipping the food in an antibiotic bath; this works well for fresh fish and meat. Of course there are also the chemical preservatives and other additives that have been used in food for some time, such as propionates to inhibit moulds in bread, anti-oxidants to slow down the process by which fats become rancid, emulsifying agents, bleaching agents, and so on.

In many other ways, some obvious and some subtle, modern food industries have contrived to reduce the attrition of food between its harvesting in the field and its delivery to the consumer. These include scientific storage at the right temperature and humidity with protection from rodents and insects, protective packaging (for which polyethylene and other synthetic wrappings have been particularly useful), and rapid transportation in refrigerated ships, cars, and airplanes. Today there is virtually no food that cannot be delivered fresh and with only minor losses to consumers everywhere.

Better food production and better food conservation are the prime requirements of the ill-fed countries. There is a third modern development that could also help them tremendously – artificial enrichment of their food with vitamins and other substances.

Everyone knows the story of the dramatic conquest of goitre in the United States and elsewhere by the simple device of adding iodine to the salt. Iodized salt in the 1920s practically eliminated goitre in the U.S. Middle West and Switzerland, where iodine is missing from the normal inland diet. In recent years Guatemala, by the iodization of salt, has abruptly reduced the incidence of goitre to less than 10 per cent in areas where it was formerly 30 to 60 per cent, and Colombia has achieved similar results. Salt iodization is now an officially sponsored practice in a number of underdeveloped countries.

Other deficiency diseases, such as pellagra and beriberi, can be eliminated by the simple addition of vitamins to wheat flour and polished rice. Here it is usually a case of restoring valuable food elements that are lost in the processing of the whole grain into the 'refined' food. Since 1941 the enrichment of wheat flour with thiamine, riboflavin, and niacin has been a general practice in the United States and Canada, and it is required by law in Puerto Rico and the Central American countries. Such legislation should be adopted by all countries depending on refined wheat flour as a basic food. The same holds for polished rice. In a test on a large scale in the Philippines from 1948 to 1950 it was shown that enrichment of polished rice with vitamins was very effective in combating beriberi in this rice-eating population. Corn meal also needs to be enriched; a diet consisting mainly of corn may produce pellagra, the disease resulting from a deficiency of the vitamin niacin combined with a diet low in the amino acid tryptophan.

Enrichment of a nation's wheat, corn, and rice with the vitamins thiamine, riboflavin, and niacin, plus calcium and iron, costs only a few cents per person per year. It would produce significant improvements in the health of most ill-fed populations, and it is strongly recommended by international health organizations.

A great part of the hungry half of the world suffers primarily from a deficiency of protein. In most vegetables and other plant foods the protein content is low in quantity and poor in quality – meaning that it is only partly metabolized by the body. High-quality protein is hard to come by. In many of the underdeveloped countries it would require the relatively wasteful allocation of land to pasture for animals, whereas it is often more efficient at present to devote the land to the direct growing of food for human beings.

Fortunately, however, low-protein foods can be enriched economically by adding a source of the missing amino acids that are essential to the synthesis of proteins by the body. The nutritive value of corn meal, for example, can be greatly improved by adding to it a supplement of 3 per cent fish flour, 3 per cent egg powder, 3 per cent food yeast, 5 per cent skim milk, 8 per cent soybean flour, or 8 per cent cottonseed flour. Any of these supplements will supply material for protein synthesis and also improve the efficiency of utilization of the protein in the corn meal.

A most promising development is the progress that is being made in the artificial synthesis of amino acids themselves. Synthetic methionine is already being fed to animals in the United States on a considerable scale. The addition of lysine to wheat flour or bread can raise the proportion of the wheat's usable protein from about a half to two thirds, and the amino acid threonine could make grain protein almost as fully usable as the proteins of meat and milk. The main problem so far is the cost of the synthetic amino acids. As more of them are synthesized and the price is brought down, these products of laboratory chemistry will make it possible to turn grain into meat for the meatless regions of the world.

Already nutritionists, using only natural sources, have concocted mixtures that can make a purely vegetarian diet richer in protein. The basic ingredients are a cereal grain, such as corn, rice, or wheat, and an oilseed meal. This meal, or flour, is made from the cakes that are left when the oil is pressed out of the seed. It is consequently less expensive than comparable animal protein, because it is a dividend remaining after sale of the oil. It generally contains about fifty per cent protein. Good sources of oilseed meal are cottonseed, soybean seeds, sesame seeds, sunflower seeds, and peanuts.

When a properly processed oilseed meal is mixed with a grain in the ratio of one part meal to two parts grain, the combination contains about twenty-five per cent protein of meat-like quality. With the addition of a small amount of yeast and vitamin A it makes a highly nutritious food. In tropical and subtropical areas it could serve as a complete basic food lacking only vitamin C (which is supplied in abundance by tropical fruits and vegetables) and sufficient calories. The latter are obtained readily from sugar, starchy vegetables, and such fruits as bananas and plantains.

Low-cost mixtures of this kind have been developed by the Institute of Nutrition of Central America and Panama. Under the generic name of Incaparina, they are already being manufactured and sold as basic foods in Guatemala, El Salvador, Mexico, and Colombia and will soon be available in other Latin-American countries. Incaparina has been found to be almost as good a protein source for young children as milk, and it has proved to be effective in preventing or curing protein malnutrition in children. Almost every region of the world either has already or can grow the raw materials for this food. The basic formula is about 55 per cent grain (corn, sorghum, rice, wheat, or whatever other cereal is available locally), 38 per cent oilseed meal, 3 per cent torula yeast, 3 per cent leaf meal (as a source of vitamin A), and 1 per cent calcium carbonate.

Many other schemes for getting more protein from plants have been studied. One on which a great deal of work has been done is the growing in liquid culture of the single-celled alga *Chlorella*. Efforts have also been made to concentrate or extract protein from grass, vegetables, cereals, and other plant materials. But so far all these investigations have been disappointing in one way or another: the food produced is either too expensive, unpalatable, or low in nutritive value.

Then there is the sea, whose tremendous population of fish and other edibles continues to excite the imagination of those concerned with the world's food problem. The main obstacle here is the cost of storing the catch of fish; such storage requires mechanical refrigeration, not generally available in the underdeveloped countries. The grinding of fish to make a protein-rich flour looks like a promising answer to this problem, but it calls for technical skill and costs more than providing protein in the form of surplus dried skim milk or oilseed meal. Moreover, large quantities of fish flour are not attractive in a basic daily diet. All in all, it must be said that sea food offers possibilities one should not neglect but that it cannot be regarded as a panacea for prompt solution of the world's food problems.

Finally, there is the dream of manufacturing completely synthetic foods at a cost low enough to end all food worries. After all, the essential nutrients man requires are basically chemicals whose formulas are well known. Most of them can be synthesized in the laboratory, either by direct chemical manipulation or with the help of micro-organisms. We already have synthetic vitamins, synthetic amino acids, hydrogenated fats, artificial flavouring and colouring agents, and so on. From a concentrate of soybean protein the skill of the food chemist can prepare a meat-like product that with proper flavouring, colouring, and moulding can pass for pressed ham or chicken.

The cost of such creations is still exorbitant. But the progress of chemistry is steadily reducing the cost, and almost certainly we shall eventually have synthetic foods that will compete in cost, palatability, and nutritive value with the products of the farm. Although that day is too far away to promise relief of the present food crisis in the underdeveloped regions, it may help to forestall the crises threatened for the future by the growth of the world's population.

Along with modern food technology go modern dangers. As man takes a more active hand in shaping and extending his food supply he introduces new hazards in what he eats – mainly potentially dangerous new food additives. Thus the safety of our food has become a paramount issue in the industrial age.

Indeed, it has always been something of an issue. We tend to overlook the fact that there are toxic substances in most of the plants we use for food, even the common ones. Fortunately they are usually eliminated or reduced to harmless proportions by cooking or other processing.

Many legumes (notably soybeans) contain an inhibitor that interferes with the action of the protein-digesting enzyme trypsin. Some also have substances that clump the red blood cells. Cabbages and several other common vegetables contain materials that deny iodine to the thyroid gland and so tend to produce goitre. Certain vegetables and cereals have high concentrations of oxalates and phytates, which bind iron and calcium and prevent the use of these minerals by the body. There are also common plants that harbour some of the deadliest poisons known to man. The cassava root contains cyanides; lima beans, the common vetch, and the broad bean have a glucoside that gives rise to cyanides; the broad bean also contains a compound that causes hemolytic anaemia; the chick-pea contains an unknown substance that produces the disease lathyrism (spastic paralysis of the legs). Consequently man has always had to be careful, and still needs to be, in his choice and processing of natural foods.

The new dangers arise from the increasing and necessary use of chemicals at all stages in the production and handling of food, from the planting of the seed to the packaging of the final product. The hazard begins with the pesticides and other poisons used to protect and promote the growth of the plant. (One may hope that another contaminant – radio-active fallout from nuclear tests – will now effectively be eliminated.) After harvesting, grain and legumes become subject to poisoning by moulds unless they are properly stored. Then there is the potential toxicity of residues of the hormones and antibiotics that have become a standard part of the feeding of meat animals. Next come the chemicals added to foods during the processing for flavour, colour, and preservative purposes. Along the way the food may pick up traces of toxic detergents that have been used to clean the tanks or containers in which it is processed. Finally, the wrappings in which the food is packaged may inadvertently add some toxic contamination.

The whole sequence is imperfectly known; no one can be quite sure just where all the dangers lurk. Gradually the advanced countries have awakened to the need for vigilance in all stages of the handling of food. With respect to the chemical treatment of foods, U.S. legislation and the policy of the Food and Drug Administration are now based on the principle that 'there are no harmless substances; there are only harmless ways of using them'.

If the technically developed countries are concerned about the safety of their food supplies, obviously the less developed ones must be even more so, as they attempt a rapid modernization of their food-producing and food-processing methods. The control of food contamination has become a world-wide problem, and the World Health Organization and the Food and Agriculture Organization of the United Nations have initiated conferences, committees, and periodic reports on control regulations in the various countries. International research and standards will be helpful, but each country must take the responsibility for guarding the safety of its own food supply.

What can be done to help the hungry half of the world pull itself up from its undernourished state and speed up the developments that would enable it to feed itself decently?

Even pessimists must note, first of all, that the prospects of the impoverished peoples are brightened by a most remarkable turn in human history. Whereas in the past men have been concerned only with feeding their own families and have fought long and bitter wars for food, we see today a new and remarkable world-wide concern for feeding the hungry wherever they are. Whether this arises out of advanced humanitarianism, the fears of the well-fed or the contest between the West and Communism is less important than the fact that the wealthy countries are taking an interest in the peoples of the poor countries.

During the past nine years the United States has sent more than $12,000 million worth of its surplus food to these countries. The Food and Agriculture Organization, at the suggestion of Canada and the United States, has launched an international effort for the same purpose with a $100 million fund as a starter, and it is now conducting a five-year Freedom from Hunger campaign.

This emergency help is not to be underestimated, and one hopes that it will be continued and even enlarged, preferably under international auspices.

A second way in which the developed countries are helping substantially is by example and by technical advice and assistance to the developing areas. The example, again, is important. The U.S. Department of Agriculture has estimated that at the present rate of progress in agricultural productivity the developed countries will be able to produce almost twice as much food as they need by the year 2000. Such an advance cannot fail to infect and stimulate the backward countries.

Yet when all is said and done, these countries must themselves generate the means for their emancipation from hunger. To do so they will have to change long-established habits and attitudes. Neither well-meant exhortations nor government decrees are likely to persuade them – certainly not in a hurry. Concrete steps may, however, speed reforms by quickly convincing the people of their value.

It is easy to list effective projects that the governments of these countries might undertake. Make available to the farmers the seeds and stocks of improved plant varieties and animal breeds. Build chemical-fertilizer plants. Supply agricultural chemicals for pest control and other special purposes. Provide new implements and machinery suitable for the local types of farming. Extend credit to the farmers for their new seeds and equipment. Pay them subsidies to start urgently needed new crops. And above all, establish training programmes that will show them how to handle their new materials and equipment and to farm more efficiently.

Education must receive the first priority for the advancement of these countries. The development of each one of the Western countries has been founded on the literacy and knowledge of its population. This applies to their progress in agriculture as well as to their achievements in industrial technology and professional services. To raise itself the underdeveloped country requires a population that understands modern agriculture and nutrition, is equipped with teachers and experts in all the fields of food technology, and is led by political and administrative officials who appreciate the possibilities of science and technology.

This will be a long and difficult programme for some of the poorly educated and ill-fed nations. But investment in education is a far more practical and effective programme for them than investment in big buildings, dams, roads, and factories that are put up mainly as visible symbols of progress. Just as the strength of the so-called developed countries lies in their educational systems and their culture, so the great hope and promise of the future for the underdeveloped countries resides in the fact that they too will come to share in the full wealth of mankind's knowledge and contribute to it themselves.

Water

ROGER REVELLE

Men need water to drink and for many other purposes, but by far the largest amount of water they have available must go to agriculture. Again, the basic need in the proper utilization of water is education.

> Did you ever hear of Sweet Betsy from Pike
> Who crossed the wide prairie with her lover Ike?
> The alkali desert was burning and bare
> And Ike got disgusted with everything there.
> They reached California with sand in their eye,
> Saying, 'Good-by Pike County, we'll stay till we die.'

This bleary and partly unprintable ballad of the 1850s marks the time when most Americans first became aware of the problems of water in national development. In northern Europe, where most of their ancestors had lived, there had always been plenty of water; in the eastern United States, where they had learned to farm, abundant rain supplied all the water needs of their crops. But when the pioneers crossed the Missouri River, they came to an arid country where water was more precious than land: its presence meant life, its absence death.

Today water problems are part of the national consciousness, and most Americans are aware that the future development of their country is intimately related to the wise use of water resources. The same obviously holds true for the less-developed countries. The water problems of the United States and the poorer countries are fundamentally similar, but they also differ in significant ways.

Water is both the most abundant and the most important substance with which man deals. The quantities of water required for his different uses vary over a wide range. The amount of drinking water needed each year by human beings and domestic animals is of the order of ten tons per ton of living tissue. Industrial water requirements for washing, cooling, and the circulation of materials range from one to two tons per ton of product in the manufacture of brick to 250 tons per ton of paper and 600 tons per ton of nitrate fertilizer. Even the largest of these quantities is small compared with the amounts of water needed in agriculture. To grow a ton of sugar or corn under irrigation, about 1,000 tons of water must be 'consumed', that is, changed by soil evaporation and plant transpiration from liquid to vapour. Wheat, rice, and cotton fibre, respectively, require about 1,500, 4,000, and 10,000 tons of water per ton of crop.

When we think of water and its uses, we are concerned with the volume of flow through the hydrologic cycle; hence the most meaningful measurements are in terms of volume per unit time: acre-feet per year, gallons per day, cubic feet per second. An acre-foot is 325,872 gallons, the amount of water required to cover an acre of land to a depth of one foot. Eleven hundred acre-feet a year is approximately equal to one million gallons a day, or 1.5 cubic feet per second. A million gallons a day fills the needs of 5,000 to 10,000 people in a city; 1,100 acre-feet a year is enough to irrigate 250 to 300 acres of farmland.

The total amount of rain and snow falling on the earth each year is about 380,000 million acre-feet: 300,000 million on the ocean and 80,000 million on the land. Over the ocean 9 per cent more water evaporates than falls back as rain. This is balanced by an equal excess of precipitation over evaporation on land; consequently the volume of water carried to the sea by glaciers, rivers, and coastal springs is close to 27,000 million acre-feet per year. About 13,000 million acre-feet is carried by 68 major river systems from a drainage area of 14,000 million acres. Somewhat less than half the run-off of liquid water from the land to the ocean is carried by thousands of small rivers flowing across coastal plains or islands; the area drained is about 11,000 million acres, but part of this is desert with virtually no run-off.

Eight thousand million acres on the continents drain into inland seas, lakes, or playas. This includes most of the earth's 6,000 million acres of desert and also such relatively well-watered areas as the basins of the Volga, Ural, Amu Darya, and Syr Darya rivers, which transport several hundred million acre-feet of water each year into the Caspian and Aral seas. The remainder of the land surface, about four thousand million acres, is covered by glaciers.

Even agriculture, man's principal consumer of water, takes little of the available supply. One thousand million acre-feet per year – less than 4 per cent of the total river flow – is used to irrigate 310 million acres of land, or about one per cent of the land area of the earth. Roughly 10,000 million acre-feet of rainfall and snowfall is evaporated and transpired each year from the remaining 3,000 million acres of the earth's cultivated lands and thus helps to grow mankind's food and fibre. Most river waters flow to the sea almost unused by man, and more than half of the water evaporating from the continents – particularly that part of the evaporation taking place in the wet rain forests and semi-humid savannas of the Tropics – plays little part in human life.

Although it is not usually reckoned as such in economic statistics, water can be considered a raw material. In the United States the production of raw materials has a minor role in the total economy, and water costs are small even when compared with those of other raw materials. The cost of all the water used by U.S. householders, industry, and agriculture is around $5,000 million a year: only 1 per cent of the gross national product. The less-developed countries, where raw materials are a major component of the economy, cannot afford water prices that would be acceptable in the United States.

In the United States, water costs $10 to $20 an acre-foot, compared with wholesale prices of $22,000 an acre-foot for petroleum, $100,000 an acre-foot for milk, and $1 million an acre-foot (not counting taxes) for bourbon whisky. The largest tanker ever built can hold less than $1,000 worth of water. Yet Americans use so much water – about 1,700 gallons a day per capita – that capital costs for water development are comparable to other kinds of investment. Although the water diverted from streams and pumped from the ground is equivalent to only about seven per cent of the rain and snow falling on the United States, this is still an enormous quantity: 200 times more than the weight of any other material used except air. The annual capital expenditure for water structures in the United States – dams, community and industrial water works, sewage-treatment plants, pipelines and drains, irrigation canals, river-control structures, and hydro-electric works – is about $10,000 million.

One of the most critical water problems of the United States is represented by the vast water-short region of the South-west and the high Western plains. In some parts of the South-west, water stored underground is being mined at an alarmingly high rate, and new sources must soon be found to supply even the present population. The average annual supply of controllable water in the entire region is 76 million acre-feet. If agriculture continued to develop at the present rate, 98 to 131 million acre-feet would be required by the year 2000. Provided that the neighbouring water-surplus regions could be persuaded to share their abundance, this deficit could be met by long-distance transportation of 22 to 55 million acre-feet per year. But the annual cost would be $2,000 million to $4,000 million, or $60 to $100 per acre-foot of water, including amortization of capital costs of $30,000 million to $70,000 million. The cost per acre-foot would be too high for most agriculture, although not too high for municipal, industrial, and recreational needs.

Nathaniel Wollman, of the University of New Mexico, and his colleagues have shown that the average value added to the economy of the South-west through the use of water in irrigation is only $44 to $51 an acre-foot, whereas the value gained from recreational uses could be about $250 an acre-foot and from industrial uses $3,000 to $4,000 an acre-foot. Because the quantities of water consumed by city-dwellers and their industries are much less than those in agriculture, the arid Western states would not require such a vast increase in future supply if they shifted from a pre-dominantly agricultural to a predominantly industrial economic base.

The value of water in the water-short regions of the United States that are in a phase of rapid economic development increases more rapidly than the cost. Even high-cost water is a small burden on the gross product of a predominantly industrial and urban economy, and high water costs are only a small economic disadvantage. This is easily overcome if other conditions, such as climate, happen to be propitious.

Throughout the country favourable benefit-to-cost ratios can usually be attained from relatively high-cost multi-purpose water developments for city residents, industry, irrigation agriculture, the oxidation and dispersal of muni-cipal and industrial wastes, the generation of hydro-electric power, pollution control, fish and wildlife conservation, navigation, recreation, and flood control.

In the less developed countries water development by itself does not produce much added value for the present economy. Municipal and industrial water requirements are much smaller than they are in the United States, and the immediate water needs are chiefly for agriculture, which calls for about the same amount of water in any warm region. Most of these countries have a low-yielding subsis-tence agriculture that brings in very little cash per acre-foot of water, and their farmers can afford to pay only a few dollars per acre-foot. Development of water resources must be accomplished by other measures to raise agricultural yields per acre-foot and per man-hour, and in general to increase the economic value of water.

One means of coping with water problems in both the United States and the less-developed countries is to improve the present rather low efficiency of water use. Here much could be done by effective research. For example, about half of the water provided for irrigation is lost in transport, and less than half of the water that reaches the fields is utilized by plants.

New mulching methods are already being applied to reduce evaporation from soil surfaces, thereby making more water available for transpiration by the plants. Through research on the physiology of water uptake and transport in plants, and on plant genetics, transpiration could probably be lowered without a proportional reduction in growth. Development of salt-tolerant crops would reduce the amounts of irrigation water needed to maintain low salt concentrations in the solution around the plant roots. The loss of water by seepage from irrigation canals and percolation from fields would be lowered by the development of better linings for canals and better irrigation practices. Losses from canals would also be reduced if we could learn how to control useless water-loving plants that suck water through the canal banks and transpire it to the air.

In arid regions the run-off from a large area must be concentrated to provide water for a relatively small fraction of the land, and techniques are needed to increase the proportion of total precipitation that can be concentrated. Development of such techniques requires research on means of increasing the run-off from mountain areas (for example, by reducing evaporation from snow fields and modifying the plant cover in order to reduce transpiration) and on methods of accelerating the rate of recharge of valley aquifers.

Finally, water problems could be dealt with by steps that – in contrast to those seeking to make better use of existing supplies – seek to increase the total volume of fresh water. Here research moves on two fronts: attempts to modify precipitation patterns by exerting control over weather and climate, and development of more economical methods of converting sea water or brackish water to fresh water. The ability to control weather and climate, even to a small degree, would be of the greatest importance to human beings everywhere. Whether or not a measure of control can be obtained will remain uncertain until we understand the natural processes in the atmosphere much better than we do now. As for desalination, this could be accomplished more economically than at present if the amount of energy required to separate water and salt could be reduced or the cost of energy lowered. Research on the properties of water, salt solutions, surfaces, and membranes is fundamental to the desalination problem. So is research aimed at lowering energy costs.

We know too little to be able to make more than a rough appraisal of the potentialities of water-resources development for agriculture in the less-developed countries. The modern technology of irrigation engineering, drainage, sanitation, and agricultural practice is quite different from that which determined patterns of land and water use in the past. At the same time technology is almost completely lacking for expanding productive agriculture in the areas of most abundant water and almost unused land: the humid Tropics. Our concern should be not only to find ways of increasing total production in order to feed and clothe the world's expanding human population but also to raise production per farm worker, that is, to raise living standards. A world-wide strategy for development of land and water will require a careful analysis of existing knowledge, region by region, together with field surveys and experimental research in each region by experienced and imaginative specialists.

In humid areas agriculture is limited only by the extent of good land; in arid lands water is the absolute limiting factor. Unless climates can be modified or sea water can be cheaply converted and economically transported, the area of arable land in the arid zone will always exceed the available water. At present, however, neither surface nor underground waters are fully utilized, either for double-cropping in presently cultivated lands or for bringing new land under cultivation.

In addition to improving the utilization of water and increasing agricultural yields, other problems that contributed to the destruction of desert civilizations in the past must still be overcome in arid land development. Among them is the fact that the spreading of water over large areas provides a fertile ground for human diseases, such as malaria and bilharzia, and for plant pests. Egyptian records show an average of one plague every eleven years. Uncontrollable malaria might well have been the cause of the mysterious disappearance of the great civilization of the cities Mohenjo-Daro and Harappa, which flourished 4,500 years ago in the Indus valley of Pakistan.

Soil drainage in a nearly level flood plain is very difficult and is usually neglected, with the result that the water table comes close to the surface and drowns the roots of most crop plants. Water rises through the soil by capillary action and evaporates, leaving an accumulation of salt that poisons the plants. The related disasters of waterlogging and salinity may have caused the ruin of the Babylonian civilization in the valley of the Tigris-Euphrates, and they are a frightening menace today in West Pakistan.

Another threat is the conflict between the sedentary farmers of the plain and the nomadic herdsmen. The present-day Powindahs of West Pakistan remind us of this ancient conflict. In our own West the feuds between cattlemen and farmers are still a vivid memory.

In considering the possibilities of agricultural development in the world's arid lands one thinks first of the famous rivers that have played so large a role in human history: among them the Nile, the Indus and its tributaries, and the Tigris-Euphrates.

For thousands of years the Egyptians carried out irrigation by allowing the Nile waters during flood stage to spread in ponded basins broadly over the delta and the valley. When the flood subsided, the basin banks were cut and the ponded water flowed back to the river. The Nile and the sun were said to be the prime farmers of Egypt. It was thought that the river's silt, deposited during the annual flood, fertilized the soil. Sun-drying and -cracking, during the fallow season before the flood, deeply furrowed the soil and killed off weeds and micro-organisms, making plough-ing unnecessary. The flood arrived in July, reached its height in September, and subsided quickly. The fields were sown in early winter with wheat, barley, beans, onions, flax, and clover. Summer crops were grown only on the river levees and in areas that contained a shallow water table, where water could be lifted by hand from the river banks or from wells. High floods left the basins pestilential morasses that brought plagues and epidemics. Low floods brought famine.

During the past one hundred and forty years this ancient system has been transformed. In 1820 Egypt had reached a nadir, with a population of only 2.5 million and with three million cultivated acres. This date marked the beginning of perennial canal irrigation and widespread planting of sum-mer crops, including cotton, corn, rice, and sugar cane as well as the traditional winter crops. Low dams called barrages were built across the river; the water backed up behind these structures was diverted through large new canals that flowed the year round. By 1955–6 the cultivated area had increased to 5.7 million acres and the intensity of cultivation to 177 per cent; that is, more than 10 million acres of crops were harvested. Salinity and waterlogging became serious menaces in the early part of this century, but they have been fairly well controlled by an extensive drainage system. Chemical fertilizers are used in large amounts and crop yields per acre are high, even though the Nile silt no longer settles on the fields but is deposited back of the barrages. Sufficient food is grown to feed the present population of 27 million. From the standpoint of crop yields per acre, although not per man, Egypt is a developed country.

The average annual flow of the Nile is 72 million acre-feet, but it is occasionally as high as 105 million acre-feet or as low as 36 million. If all the average flow could be utilized, it would be enough to irrigate 12 to 15 million acres on a year-round basis. At present the area of irrigated land in Egypt is less than half that. During the flood season much of the water flows to the sea unused, and during the rest of the year a shortage of surface and underground water limits the size of the cultivated area.

Now the construction of the Aswan High Dam promises to bring the river under complete control. The dam will have a storage capacity of 105 million acre-feet, equal to the highest annual flow during the past century. There will no longer be a Nile flood; the tamed river will become simply a huge feeder canal for irrigation. With the average of 55 million acre-feet per year available to Egypt (17 million acre-feet from the reservoir is allocated to the Sudan), it will be possible to increase the cultivated area in the delta and the valley floor by 2.2 million acres, or nearly 40 per cent, and to convert 0.7 million acres from flood to perennial irrigation. Hydro-electric power generation of more than a million kilowatts will make power available for pump drainage, which may increase crop production by 20 per cent, and for the manufacture of chemical fertilizers. The electric power will also be used to lift water to the desert margins of the valley, where it is hoped that an additional one to two million acres can be brought under the plough. If all these benefits can be realized, total agricultural production in Egypt can be increased by 90 per cent, enough to feed almost twice the present population and at the same time provide crops for export.

When Alexander the Great pushed his tired armies eastward some 2,300 years ago, they came at last to an old desert civilization on the banks of the mightiest river they had ever seen. The Aryans, who had preceded Alexander by 1,000 years, did not give the river a name; they called it simply the 'Indus', which was their word for river, and they named the subcontinent they had invaded 'India': the land of the river.

The Indus and its five tributaries of the Punjab, together with the flat plain through which they flow, are one of the major natural resources of the earth. In the Punjab and Sind regions of West Pakistan 30 million persons dwell on the plain; 23 million make their living from farming it. They produce most of the food and fibre that feed and clothe nearly 50 million people.

The rivers carry more than twice the flow of the Nile. Half this water is diverted into a highly developed system of irrigation canals and is used to irrigate some 23 million acres – by far the largest single irrigation region on earth. Underneath the northern part of the plain lies a huge reservoir of fresh ground water, equal in volume to ten times the annual flow of the rivers.

In spite of the great potentialities of the plain, the fact is that poverty and hunger, not well-fed prosperity, are today the common lot of the people of West Pakistan. These afflictions are nowhere more desperately evident than in the farming villages of the countryside. In a country of farmers food must be imported to provide the most meagre of diets; the gap between food production and the number of mouths to be fed is widening.

The problem of agriculture in West Pakistan is both a physical and a human one. It is a problem of land, water, and people and of the interactions among them. One of its aspects is the waterlogging and salt accumulation in the soil, caused by poor drainage in the vast, nearly flat plain, that are slowly destroying the fertility of much of the irrigated land. The area of canal-irrigated and cultivated land already seriously damaged by waterlogging and salinity is close to five million acres, or about eighteen per cent of the gross sown area. Three other difficulties also beset agriculture: shortage of irrigation water, problems of land tenure, and poor farming practices.

Although crops can be grown throughout the year, and both a winter and a summer growing season are traditional, the irrigation canals lose so much water by seepage that the amount carried to the fields is sufficient to irrigate only about half the land during each season. Even so, the crops are inadequately irrigated, particularly in summer. Much of the cropped area receives insufficient water to prevent salt accumulation.

Many of the farmers are share-cropping tenants who have little incentive to increase production. Nearly all of them struggle with small and widely separated plots that multiply the difficulties of efficient use of irrigation water and farm animals and gravely inhibit change in traditional practices.

In West Pakistan we have the wasteful paradox of a great and modern irrigation system pouring its water onto lands cultivated as they were in the Middle Ages. Ploughing is done by a wooden plough of ancient design, pulled by undernourished bullocks. Unselected seeds are sown broadcast. Pakistan uses only a hundredth as much fertilizer per acre as Egypt.

Careful investigation shows that in most of the Punjab the problems of waterlogging and salinity could be cured, and at the same time adequate water could be supplied to the crops, by sinking fields of large wells to pump the underground water and spread it on the cultivated lands. Part of the pumped water would be carried off by evaporation and transpiration and part would percolate back into the ground, in the process washing the salt out of the soil.

If the well fields are too small in area, lateral infiltration of underground water from the surrounding land will be large compared with the rate at which the pumped water can evaporate, and the process of dewatering will be retarded or completely inhibited. For this and other reasons each Punjab project area should be about a million acres in size.

Removal of salt and provision of additional water are necessary, but by no means sufficient, measures to raise agriculture in West Pakistan from its desperate poverty. Equally essential are chemical fertilizers, higher yielding seeds, pest control, credit and marketing facilities, and above all incentives and knowledge to adopt better farming practices. The job cannot be done all at once; it is necessary to concentrate on project areas of manageable size. Initial capital costs for a million-acre project in the Punjab would be about $55 million, including costs of wells and electrification, nitrogen-fertilizer plants, pest-control facilities, and filling of administrative, educational, and research pipelines.

In the Sind region initial capital costs would be considerably higher, probably between $130 million and $165 million per million acres. That is largely because the underground water in most of the Sind is too salty to be used for irrigation, and drainage is therefore a more difficult matter than in the Punjab.

After a few years the minimum net increase in crop value in each million-acre project in the Punjab could be $55 million to $60 million a year, equal to the capital costs and to twice the present gross production, excluding livestock. In the Sind the net increase, including livestock, could probably be at least equal to the present output.

The same interrelated problems of water, land, and people that afflict the Indus plain also exist in the valley of the Tigris-Euphrates, but on a much smaller scale. Salty soil is found over large areas; because of waterlogging it is possible to cultivate only about a third of the seven million acres of irrigated land each year. The remainder is left fallow and unirrigated to dry out the subsoil and to build up a little soil nitrogen. Great damage was done long ago when the ancient canal systems were destroyed and the land was depopulated by waves of nomadic invaders. But the nomads merely hastened the salt accumulation and waterlogging that were the seeds of destruction. These had begun centuries earlier as a result of inadequate draining and inability to control floods.

If the flow of the Tigris-Euphrates could be fully utilized, through combined development of surface and ground water, and if the soils were adequately leached and drained, the irrigated area cultivated each year could be increased to 10 to 12 million acres. If greater water usage were combined with perennial cropping, better farming practices, and the application of chemical fertilizers, total agricultural production could be raised at least fivefold.

The largest opportunities for expansion of the area of irrigated arid and semiarid lands exist in the U.S.S.R. Between 1950 and 1960, 15 million acres in the neighbourhood of the Black and Caspian seas were provided with irrigation water from the Volga, Dnieper, Amu Darya, and Syr Darya rivers. The total flow of these rivers is more than 300 million acre-feet, sufficient, under the cold-winter and warm-summer climate of the steppes, to supply all the water needed to irrigate 70 to 100 million acres.

Because of the relatively advanced level of the country, large multipurpose water developments in the U.S.S.R. are economically feasible, and a high percentage of the capital invested goes for power, transportation, industrial water supplies, and flood control.

Soviet engineers have outlined a plan to build an immense dam on the Ob River, creating an inland sea five sixths the size of Italy, and to dig a canal connecting the Yenisei with the Ob above the dam. The impounded waters would be transported through a giant system of canals, rivers, and lakes to the Aral Sea and thence by canal to the Caspian Sea. Several hundred million acre-feet of water that now goes to waste each year in the Arctic Ocean would be conserved. This water would be used to irrigate 50 million acres of crop lands and a somewhat larger area of pasture in arid western Siberia and Kazakhstan. Accompanying hydro-electric power installations would have a capacity of more than 70 million kilowatts. Major storage, irrigation, and hydro-electric works are also under construction or planned in the northern Caucasus and in the Azerbaijan, Georgian, and Armenian Soviet Socialist republics. These will bring additional tens of millions of acres under irrigation.

In some parts of the arid zone both surface and ground water are so scarce that it is difficult to see how irrigation agriculture can be developed to support the rapidly expanding population. In the Maghreb countries of North Africa – Tunisia, Algeria, and Morocco – there is probably not enough water in the region north of the Sahara to irrigate more than 3.5 million acres of land, yet the combined population of these three countries is already 26 million (equal to Egypt's) and will double in twenty to twenty-five years. Elaborate systems of dry farming have been developed in the Maghreb; for example, the planting of olive trees far apart in light, sandy soils that catch and hold the night-time dew. With this technique it has been possible to grow olive and other fruit trees on more than a million acres in Tunisia. In the long run it may be necessary to employ most of the available water in the Maghreb countries for industrial purposes, because these can provide a tenfold to hundredfold higher marginal value for water than agriculture can.

A new possibility for water development has recently been opened, however. During the past few years evidence has been obtained that large areas in the Sahara may be underlain by an enormous lake of fresh water. In some places the water-bearing sands are 3,000 feet thick, and they appear to extend for at least 500 miles south of the Atlas Mountains and perhaps eastward into Tunisia and Libya. If this evidence is correct, the amount of useful water may be very large indeed – of the order of 100,000 million acre-feet, sufficient to irrigate many millions of acres for centuries.

In general the possibilities of expanding the area of irrigated land in the arid zone outside the U.S.S.R. are not large when measured in numbers of acres. But crop yields under irrigation in the arid lands are high and assured if all the factors of agricultural production are properly applied. In fact, irrigation agriculture in arid regions can be successful only if it is intensive and high-yielding; it is costly to construct and maintain draining systems that will keep the water table from rising too close to the surface, and to provide enough water on each acre to leach the salts out of the soil. In hot, arid lands some kinds of irrigation agriculture can be so productive that very expensive irrigation water, such as could be produced by sea-water desalination, may soon become economical.

Much greater possibilities (and also greater difficulties) exist for agricultural expansion in the regions of savanna climate, which are characterized by an annual cycle of heavy rainfall during one season, followed by drought the remainder of the year, and by warm weather at all seasons. In Africa, for example, many millions of what are now barren acres could be brought under irrigated cultivation, provided that interested farmers could be found, in the neighbourhood of the great bend of the Niger River in former French West Africa, in the basin of the Rufiji River of Tanganyika, and near Lake Kyoga in Uganda. Similarly, in the area extending from India east through Burma, Thailand, and Vietnam to the northern Philippines, air temperature and solar radiation are suitable for year-round crop growth, and water and land are the limiting factors.

In the lower basin of the Ganges and Brahmaputra rivers, comprising East Pakistan and the Indian states of Bengal, Bihar, and Assam, some 140 million people live on 70 million cultivated acres. The basic resources of soil and water are grossly under-utilized in this land of ancient civilization, extreme present poverty, and strong population pressure. Each year the rivers carry about 1,000 million acre-feet to the Bay of Bengal, and in the process they flood most of the countryside. Yet only one crop is grown a year. The land is left idle half the year because of the shortage of water, and there is a lack of useful occupation for the people six to eight months of the year. Agricultural practices are adjusted to the rhythm of the monsoon.

The opportunities for increasing production are enormous in this region of land shortage and overabundant water. Through surface and underground storage of a portion of the flood waters, water could be provided for three crops each year over more than half of the cultivable area in the alluvial plain, and a considerable additional area could receive sufficient water for two crops. An assured year-round water supply would also provide favourable conditions for intensive use of fertilizers, higher yielding plant varieties, and better farming practices, which could result in a tripling of yields per crop and per acre for cereals, pulses (the edible seeds of leguminous plants such as peas and beans), and oilseeds.

A well-fed livestock industry could be developed in addition to improvements in field crops, and a balanced diet, instead of the present completely inadequate one, could be provided for twice the present population. Expansion of agricultural production here, based on irrigation, would raise few basic problems of land and settlement, but it would require a reorientation of thinking regarding patterns of land and water use. Because of the enormous volumes of water involved and the flatness of the alluvial basin, the cost of water storage and distribution and of flood control and drainage would be high, but the returns through increased farm and livestock production could be several times higher than the cost. The yields per worker must also be increased, however, and a large degree of industrialization accomplished if the project is to finance itself.

Development of water resources is not an end in itself. The investment can be justified only if it leads to higher agricultural or industrial production, or in other ways to an increase of human well-being. To gain these objectives water development must be accompanied by other actions needed to use the water effectively. This is well illustrated in agriculture. One of the basic principles of agricultural science is the principle of interaction: the concurrent use of all the factors of production on the same parcel of land, which will give a much larger harvest than if these factors are used separately on different parcels. Adequate water and water at the right time are essential if seeds of a particular crop variety planted in a given soil are to yield a good crop. But a much larger crop is possible if seeds of a higher yield variety are planted. This potential increase in the harvest will be realized, however, only if the soil contains sufficient plant nutrients. Usually nitrogen fertilizers and phosphate fertilizers must be added in large amounts to provide the maximum yield. Increased soil fertility will be drained off by weeds unless these are rigorously controlled, and an eager host of insect pests and plant diseases will fight to share the crop with the farmer unless he can combat them with pest-control measures. Improved seed varieties planted without adequate water, abundant fertilizer, and rigorous pest control may not do even as well as the traditionally planted varieties. The potentialities for double- or triple-cropping in a perennial irrigation system cannot be achieved if the farmers do not have tractors and efficient tools to enable them to prepare their fields in the short interval between harvest and planting.

To meet the cost of new irrigation systems the farmer must produce much more per acre-foot of water than he has in the past, and this can be done only if all the factors of production are made available to him and if he is taught how to use them effectively. The human, educational, social, and institutional problems of bringing the necessary knowledge to millions of farmers are immense. The task of remaking methods of production that are intimately tied to ways of living and of overcoming institutional and political resistance to change is more difficult than any of the engineering problems. Illiteracy, malnutrition, and disease; poverty so harsh that the farmer does not dare risk innovation because failure will mean starvation; small and fragmented farm holdings; land-rental and -taxation systems that destroy incentive; extreme difficulties in obtaining a farm loan promptly at a reasonable interest rate; poor marketing and storage systems; administrative inefficiency and corruption; the shortage of trained teachers and farm advisers;

inadequate government services for agricultural research, education, and extension and for control of water-borne diseases – all must be overcome if investments in water resources in the developing countries are to produce really beneficial results.

Energy*

SAM H. SCHURR

Modern man has made himself largely by burning fuel. The supply of fuel appears to be almost inexhaustible, and a high level of fuel consumption is not a prerequisite of development but a result of it.

There is an obvious connexion between economic development and the increased use of energy from mineral sources. According to plausible estimates world consumption of mineral fuels between now and the end of the century will equal about three times the amount consumed in all previous history. Since mineral fuels are depletible resources unequally distributed around the world, it is easy to see why there should be a nagging concern about the ability of the world's resources to meet estimated future consumption.

In this chapter estimates of future world energy consumption will be compared with the availability of the natural resources from which the supplies must come. Some of the uncertainties that enter into estimates of fuel resources will be examined, and it will be indicated why some estimates are higher than others. Regardless of the discrepancy between particular estimates there is reason to be optimistic about the world outlook for fossil-fuel supplies. The outlook is made even more promising, of course, by the advent of nuclear power. Moreover, the enormous energy yield of nuclear fuels per unit of weight suggests that unique economic effects will result from the exploitation of nuclear power.

For the purpose of adding together the different energy sources, their inherent energy value can be translated into

*The following staff members of Resources for the Future, Inc., helped in the preparation of this article: Perry D. Teitelbaum, Jaroslav G. Polach, and David B. Brooks.

various common denominators, such as kilowatt-hours, calories or British thermal units. Here the practice of the United Nations will be followed and the various energy sources will be converted into 'hard-coal equivalents' (h.c.e.). In making this conversion for crude oil, refinery losses are taken into account and certain non-fuel products, such as asphalt and lubricating oil, are subtracted. Hydro-electric energy is converted to h.c.e. according to the actual energy content of a kilowatt-hour. (Prior to 1955 U.N. statistics used a conversion factor that reflected how much coal would be needed to produce a kilowatt-hour of electricity. This gave an h.c.e. three or four times higher than the h.c.e. now used for hydro-electric power.)

In 1960, according to U.N. statistics, the world's consumption of mineral fuels and hydro-electric power was 4,235 million metric tons h.c.e. (A metric ton is 1,000 kilograms, or 2,205 pounds.) On a per capita basis this amounts to about 1,400 kilograms h.c.e. The world average conceals an enormous variation among countries. At one extreme the United States, with only 6 per cent of the world's population, consumed more than a third of the world's total commercial energy supplies. Towards the other end of the range India, with almost 15 per cent of the world's population, used only about 1.5 per cent of the world's commercial energy. (The figures exclude such 'non-commercial' energy sources as wood, animal power, and dung, which constitute a significant fraction of all the energy used in India and other underdeveloped countries.) Translated into per capita terms, the average American consumed the equivalent of about 8,000 kilograms (8 metric tons) of coal per year, or more than fifty times the Indian per capita consumption.

In order to study these figures, let us divide the nations into three major groups. The first group consists of the most highly developed non-Communist nations: those of North America, western Europe, and Oceania (essentially Australia and New Zealand). The second group is made up of the U.S.S.R. and the other European Communist-bloc countries. The third group, composed overwhelmingly of the less-developed lands, consists of the nations of Asia, Africa, Latin America, and the Middle East. Half of all the energy consumed in 1960 by the third group is accounted for by Communist Asia (chiefly mainland China). The reported per capita energy consumption of 600 kilograms h.c.e. for Communist Asia seems rather high in the light of earlier Chinese figures. If China is excluded, the per capita consumption for the third group is about 315 kilograms h.c.e., compared with about 415 kilograms when China is included. For the second group the per capita energy consumption is about 2,900 kilograms h.c.e., and for the first group (which includes the United States) the figure is about 4,500.

It is scarcely surprising that there is a strong positive correlation between per capita energy consumption and per capita share of gross national product (G.N.P.). This correlation for forty-seven nations in 1961 extends and brings up to date a chart that Edward S. Mason, of Harvard University, originally prepared with 1952 figures. In presenting his chart, which used national income rather than G.N.P., Mason pointed to the inadequacies of energy statistics in many countries and to the difficulties involved in trying to reduce the per capita income figures of different countries to their equivalent in U.S. dollars. He concluded nevertheless that 'large differences in income are associated with large differences in energy intake, and we may take it for granted that no country at this stage of history can enjoy a high per capita income without becoming an extensive consumer of energy'.

Over the past three decades there has been a striking shift in the relative importance of various energy sources. In 1929 solid fuels supplied almost 80 per cent of the world's commercial energy. In 1960 the solid-fuel fraction had declined to barely half. In the same period the share supplied by liquid fuels more than doubled, from about 15

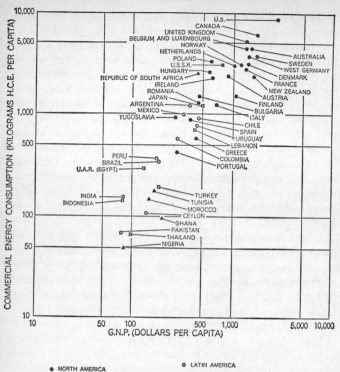

ENERGY USE *v.* G.N.P. (Gross National Product) on a per capita basis is shown for 1961. This chart is based on U.N. energy statistics and G.N.P. figures prepared largely by the Agency for International Development. For Communist countries G.N.P. is an estimate based on a report by the Centre for International Studies at the Massachusetts Institute of Technology. A similar chart for steel consumption is on page 110.

to 31 per cent. The biggest gain of all was made by natural gas, which soared from 4.5 to 14.6 per cent of the total. The share supplied by hydro-electric power more than doubled

94

during the period, but it continued to be a small fraction of the total.

The United States led the way in the shift from solid to liquid and gaseous fuels and strongly influenced world totals. In the United States oil and natural gas now supply nearly 75 per cent of all the energy consumed. In western Europe, where coal is still pre-eminent, the rise in oil consumption has been comparatively recent. In 1929 only 3.8 per cent of Europe's energy came from oil; by 1960 the figure had climbed to 30.2 per cent. The less-developed part of the world depends on oil for more than half of its total commercial supplies compared with about 30 per cent in 1929. In good part the world-wide swing to liquid fuels reflects the fact that oil can be transported much more cheaply than coal over long distances. The rapidly increasing consumption of oil makes it more urgent than ever to have good estimates of world reserves of petroleum, traditionally regarded as far below coal in abundance.

If energy consumption in the future merely maintained the per capita rate of 1960, it would place a tremendous drain on the world's energy resources. The present world population is about three thousand million. By the year 2000 the population is expected to more than double, reaching a figure of six or seven thousand million. Obviously energy consumption is destined to climb even more steeply as per capita consumption continues to rise in the highly developed regions of the world, and even more swiftly in the developing ones. The job of producing a reasonable estimate of world energy consumption over the next forty years is both formidable and hazardous.

In my opinion the most satisfactory technique for estimating world totals would be to project for each country (or region) the anticipated growth of each energy-consuming sector of the economy: industry, transportation, households, agriculture, and so on. Unfortunately the data needed to make such a detailed projection are available only for the highly developed countries.

Under the circumstances one must fall back on less satisfactory methods of estimating the world's energy needs. Of the various projections available I prefer to use those prepared for the U.S. Atomic Energy Commission by Milton F. Searl. His estimates are reasonably detailed and allow for different rates of growth in different regions of the world. Moreover, Searl's projections of world energy consumption through the remainder of this century are the highest made by any serious student of the problem. It seems desirable to use a reasonably high estimate because it offers a severe test for the measurement of the adequacy of resources.

Searl's projections of world energy consumption and population in 1980 and 2000 are compared with 1960 figures. By the year 2000 a world population twice that of 1960 will consume about five times more energy. At that date the countries of North America, western Europe, and Oceania will account for only 45 per cent of the world total, compared with almost 60 per cent in 1960. Over the same period the share of the U.S.S.R. and eastern Europe will decline slightly from about 21 per cent to 19. Meanwhile energy consumption in the rest of the world will have climbed from about 20 per cent of the world total in 1960 to about 35 per cent in the year 2000.

Part of the energy rise in Asia, Africa, Latin America, and the Middle East will be accounted for by a rise in population from about 72 per cent of the world total in 1960 to about 77 per cent in 2000. In the main, however, the under-developed countries' increased share of projected world energy is accounted for by the assumption that they will be building up an industrial base between 1960 and 2000.

The experience of the United States in energy consumption provides support for this assumption. In five of the six decades from 1850 to 1910 – a period during which this country was building its industrial base – the average annual increase in the per capita consumption of mineral fuels and hydro-electric power was around 5 per cent, whereas in subsequent decades the rate fell substantially. Per capita consumption of commercial energy in the underdeveloped world in 1960 (414 kilograms h.c.e.) is about the level reached in the United States somewhere between 1850 and 1855 – more than one hundred years earlier. The per capita energy consumption estimated for the underdeveloped world in 2000 (about 1,500 kilograms h.c.e.) was reached in the U.S. around 1880. It happens that Searl's projections for the year 2000 were made without special reference to the U.S. record in the nineteenth century. It is interesting to note, therefore, that his estimates for the progress to be made in the underdeveloped world in the last part of the twentieth century closely parallel the U.S. experience in the latter part of the nineteenth century.

There is another parallel in energy consumption between the United States of one hundred years ago and the underdeveloped world of today: the heavy consumption of noncommercial fuels. As late as 1870 wood accounted for about three quarters of the total U.S. energy consumption. By 1910 wood's share had fallen to about 10 per cent of the total. In a careful study of India's energy consumption in 1959 it was found that non-commercial fuels (excluding animal power) accounted for about 70 per cent of the country's total energy supply. Almost all the non-commercial fuels were consumed in households. The transformation in energy use that took place in the United States in the second half of the past century can be expected to take place in India and elsewhere during the latter half of this one.

Are world energy resources adequate to the expected demand? According to Searl's estimates, between 1960 and 2000 the world will have consumed the equivalent of about 435,000 million metric tons of coal. More than half of the total, about 225,000 million tons, will have been consumed in North America, western Europe, and Oceania; more than a quarter, about 120,000 million tons, in the less-developed countries; the remainder, about 90,000 million tons, in the U.S.S.R. and eastern Europe. The cumulative total is slightly more than 100 times the world's 1960 rate of consumption, which means in turn that over the forty-year period the world's energy resources will be depleted at an average annual rate 2.5 times that of 1960.

In appraising the adequacy of world resources one can neglect hydro-electric power because of its surprisingly small importance. It can be significant, however, in the energy supply of particular countries. Solar radiation, although it is a vast and for all practical purposes an inexhaustible source of energy, will be omitted from this discussion because no way has yet been found to use it as an economic substitute for commercial fuels on a major scale. Its greatest promise appears to lie in small-scale applications, such as household cooking and water-heating – the very applications in which non-commercial fuels are so widely used today in the underdeveloped regions. Other unconventional energy sources such as geothermal and tidal power and the wind are also omitted for lack of evidence that they can add significantly to the world's energy supply over the next several decades.

One might think that in turning from estimates of energy demand to the question of the adequacy of resources one would be leaving conjecture behind and entering the realm of hard geological fact. Actually there is no true measure of the world's endowment of energy resources, nor, in the nature of things, is there ever likely to be one. Cost alone would prohibit a comprehensive probing of the earth's crust to provide anything approaching a true measure of resources. More to the point, society's interest is confined to resources that are exploitable now or seem likely to be in the future. As time passes, the standards of exploitability keep changing, mainly as a result of advances in technology and changes in economic circumstances. Consequently resource-supply estimates are subject to at least as many uncertainties as energy-demand estimates. Although resource estimates embody some actual measurements of the contents of known deposits, they are based chiefly on geological inference.

Let us first consider coal. Estimates of total resources will differ, depending on such factors as the maximum depth of coal beds to be included, their minimum thickness, and whether or not the estimator is willing to include undiscovered deposits whose existence can be inferred. Fortunately the differences in recent estimates are not crucial, because even the most conservative ones indicate that world coal resources are enough to meet world energy needs far into the future.

The estimate of world coal resources that will be used here was compiled recently by Paul Averitt, of the U.S. Geological Survey. It shows a world total of 2,320,000 million metric tons of recoverable coal in known deposits with seams 14 inches or more thick and lying within 3,000 feet of the surface. Recoverability is estimated at 50 per cent of the coal in place, which is more or less consistent with current underground mining experience in the United States.

This is a conservative estimate in terms of its depth limitations and also in that it makes no allowance for undiscovered deposits, even within these limitations. Nevertheless, it includes far more coal than has actually been measured and great quantities of coal in deposits that would not be considered economic by current standards. Stated briefly, it is a conservative measure of the coal that is available in the earth for man to extract, if needed, by employing suitable technical and managerial ingenuity. For the purpose of comparison, a less conservative estimate made by other workers of the U.S. Geological Survey yields a world total that is seven times Averitt's estimate. The higher estimate employs the same depth and thickness limitations but allows for the discovery of new coal deposits.

If Averitt's estimate is accepted, coal could supply the entire 435,000 million tons of coal equivalent the world is expected to consume between 1960 and 2000, and enough coal would still remain in the ground at the end of the period to satisfy the world's total demands for energy for almost another century at the estimated annual level of consumption in the year 2000. If present trends continue, of course, coal will be wanted for considerably less than half of the world's energy consumption in the years ahead. The huge coal reserve is reassuring, nevertheless, because with few exceptions coal, used as such or in the generation of electricity, could be satisfactorily substituted for oil and gas in most applications, although perhaps at some added cost. And if a serious pinch were to develop in oil supplies, coal could be converted, at a price, into liquid motor fuels. However, in the United States at least, oil shale would probably be used rather than coal as a substitute oil source.

In considering resources of oil and gas one encounters a category that has no exact counterpart in world coal statistics: the concept of 'proved reserves'. The term refers to discovered and well-delineated reserves that can be extracted by available techniques at current costs and sold at current prices. Present proved reserves of oil are nearly 320,000 million barrels, equivalent to 56,000 million tons of hard coal, or more than 40 times the world-wide consumption of oil in 1960.

Proved-reserve figures, however, do not begin to provide a full accounting of oil and gas resources even in well-established oil regions. The reason is that reserves cannot be proved without drilling wells, and wells are costly. Reserves are only proved, therefore, in response to explicit commercial needs. In the United States, for example, proved reserves are essentially a working inventory of natural stocks. Consequently proved-reserve figures – which indicate that U.S. reserves will last for perhaps twelve years – are virtually useless for an analysis of the long-term adequacy of resources.

A study of the relation between world oil production, proved reserves, and addition to reserves over the period from 1950 to 1962 shows that cumulative oil production over the twelve-year period practically equalled the proved reserves existing at the start of the period but that in the meantime much larger quantities of oil resources were added to proved reserves.

For both oil and natural gas, therefore, it is necessary to estimate 'unproved' resources to obtain a figure comparable to that presented for world coal resources. Estimates of such unproved resources have generally been revised upward over the years, but even today there are wide differences on the subject.

The extremes among responsible authorities are represented by the estimates of M. King Hubbert, of the Shell Development Company, who recently completed a study of energy resources for the National Academy of Sciences, and those of Alfred D. Zapp, of the U.S. Geological Survey. Hubbert's estimate of ultimate world reserves of crude oil is 1,250,000 million barrels; Zapp's estimate of potential oil resources is about 3.5 times that, or more than 4,000,000 million barrels.

The difference in these two estimates results wholly from the widely different estimates made by the two men of the potential oil resources of the United States. Hubbert's figure for the United States is 175,000 million barrels of ultimate reserves, whereas Zapp's estimate is between 500,000 million and 600,000 million barrels. In each case the world figure is derived from the U.S. estimate by applying certain factors indicating the relative geological favourability of oil occurrence in the United States and other parts of the world.

The wide gulf separating the Hubbert and Zapp evaluations of the potential oil resources of the United States (and, by extension, the world) results essentially from the different views they hold concerning the relevant variables for assessing unproved oil resources. Hubbert's approach yields an estimate that is shaped by existing economic, technical, and political factors affecting the actual production of oil in the United States. Zapp's approach yields an estimate that admittedly includes deposits that are submarginal by today's standards and whose exploitation would depend on significant improvements in exploration and production technology and perhaps increases in the price of oil.

On the basis of their estimates for oil Hubbert and Zapp were also able to make estimates of the unproved resources of natural gas (and natural-gas liquids). The resulting totals for the world's potential resources of oil and gas, expressed in hard-coal equivalents, are about 535,000 million metric tons (Hubbert) and about 1,620,000 million metric tons (Zapp).

These various estimates are not to be taken literally. No one really knows what the world's potential resources of coal, oil, and gas are. My own guess is that the estimates will be revised upward in the future if the demand for these energy sources continues to justify the search for new deposits and the development of new technology. Improved recovery technology alone could raise the figures by a considerable percentage. For example, only about a third of the oil contained in underground reservoirs in the United States is now recovered, and this low recovery factor is built into Hubbert's estimate of ultimate reserves.

In addition to coal, oil, and natural gas the earth's crust contains vast potential resources of oil shale and oil-bearing tar sands. The U.S. Geological Survey has estimated, for example, that the recoverable energy content of U.S. oil-shale resources is about a third of the total energy content of the known and inferred coal resources of the United States. There is, therefore, reason to believe that even without atomic energy the world resource base of fossil fuels would be ample into the quite distant future.

Unfortunately a particular country may find small comfort in estimates of vast world resources of fuels if the supply inside or near its own borders is scanty or non-existent. A striking aspect of the distribution of both coal and oil is their high concentration in just a few of the world's regions. In the case of coal the United States, the U.S.S.R., China, and Europe account for more than 90 per cent of the world's estimated recoverable resources; all the other regions of the world combined – which include all the underdeveloped world except China – contain only 7 per cent of known resources. For oil, four regions – the Middle East, the United States, the U.S.S.R., and Caribbean America – also possess about 90 per cent of the world's proved reserves. Most of Africa (outside of North Africa), most of South America, and India contain neither coal resources nor proved oil reserves in sizeable amounts. It is clear that the distribution of coal and oil is far from evenly matched with the distribution of the population.

Of course, the location of today's known deposits is not identical with what may be found in the future, particularly as the search for fuel resources is widened. But even if important new discoveries are made, international trade in coal and oil will continue to be important in the years ahead, and to expand in volume. The overwhelming importance of western Europe as a fuel-importing area and of the Middle East as an exporting area is clearly apparent: each accounts for about 50 per cent of the world's gross interregional imports and exports respectively. This is a comparatively recent development associated with the postwar shift towards oil in western Europe's energy consumption.

In looking to the future it is apparent that the quantitative preponderance of the developed countries as importers will continue. But as the years pass the less-developed areas of the world will be forced to increase their imports of fuels at a rapid rate. Barring discovery of local energy sources, many countries will find themselves faced with staggering bills for imported fuels.

In order to ascertain how big these bills may be my associates and I have made a rough estimate of the volume of imported fuel that will be needed in the year 2000 by underdeveloped non-Communist countries not now self-sufficient in energy. Coal imports were omitted from the calculations because oil is the preferred imported fuel of underdeveloped regions. In 1960 imported oil accounted for about 55 per cent of the total energy consumption of the non-self-sufficient countries of Latin America and Africa and for about 25 per cent in Asia. We assumed that imported oil would constitute the same percentage of energy needs in the year 2000. This estimated volume was then multiplied by current prices of crude oil (even though refined oil products would presumably account for much of the importation).

The conservative figure that resulted from this calculation was an imported-oil fuel bill in the year 2000 of about $10,000 million (at today's prices). In 1960 the same group of countries paid out only $17,000 million for imported commodities of all kinds, of which oil imports (calculated as crude oil) would have cost less than $1,000 million. It is evident from these rough figures that paying for imported-fuel supplies in 2000 may pose a difficult problem for developing countries. Although these countries can expect a growing income from exports, export earnings still may not be sufficient to pay for sharply enlarged energy imports along with imports of other necessities. International arrangements for easing the foreign-exchange burden may be needed if energy-consumption levels such as those estimated here are to be achieved.

Finally we come to the role that may be played by nuclear power in satisfying the world demand for energy. From the estimates of fossil-fuel reserves already presented it is clear that during the rest of this century and well into the next the world could get along quite well without atomic energy. Nevertheless, as nuclear power costs decline, nuclear fuels will compete increasingly with fossil fuels.

In the United States alone the potential (known and unknown) uranium resources, comparable in quality to ore now being mined, are estimated by workers of the U.S. Geological Survey to range from 2,100,000 million to 6,900,000 million tons of coal equivalents. The larger figure is substantially greater than the combined total of the world's known resources of recoverable coal and potential resources of oil and natural gas. It can be inferred from the U.S. figures that the world resources of uranium (and of thorium, which is probably more abundant than uranium) are greater than the resources of fossil fuels by an enormous margin. If much-lower-grade resources – including ordinary granite – are taken into account, man can be said to have within reach an almost unlimited supply of energy. Underlying these calculations is the assumption that through the development of the 'breeder' reactor it will be possible to convert the 'fertile' materials uranium-238 (the abundant isotope of natural uranium) and thorium-232 respectively into fissionable plutonium-239 and uranium-233.

It is difficult to estimate what effects commercial atomic energy will have on the market for conventional fuels in the years ahead. Within the past year estimates pertaining to the United States have appeared in a report to the President prepared by the Atomic Energy Commission. This report predicted that atomic power would become competitive with conventional sources of power throughout most of the United States in the 1970s, and by 1980 would generate nearly 10 per cent of the nation's electricity. It predicted further that by the end of the century all new electric power plants, and half of all the electricity then being generated in this country, would be nuclear. But it should be kept in mind that these estimates were contained in a report attempting to justify a programme of research, development, and construction that is designed to improve nuclear technology and to bring down costs. Moreover, the report made assumptions about the future costs of fossil fuels that seem unreasonably high.

But even with these reservations it is apparent that nuclear fuels will emerge as a formidable competitor of the fossil fuels, both at home and abroad. It is therefore worth speculating about the broader economic significance of atomic energy, particularly for the underdeveloped countries. The unique promise of atomic energy is inherent in the fact that nuclear fuels contain an enormous concentration of energy per unit of weight. One pound of nuclear fuel, fully consumed, is the energy equivalent of about three million pounds of coal. Several unusual economic characteristics follow from this fact. Nuclear fuels, for one thing, are essentially weightless and thus freight-free. Their employment should therefore lead towards the geographic equalization of energy costs. This may make it possible for underdeveloped countries to undertake a new pattern of economic development in which certain industries are located near existing agricultural settlements instead of being concentrated in a few large urban centres. Because nuclear fuels are freight-free they might also reduce the need for investment in railroads or pipelines, thereby conserving scarce capital. Finally, there is the long-run promise that nuclear fuels will help to reduce the foreign-exchange burden faced by fuel-poor countries.

Unfortunately the inherent advantages of nuclear fuels are counterbalanced by the present need for very large-scale installations if power is to be produced at a reasonable cost. Installations of the size needed require the prior existence of a highly concentrated market for power. Moreover, nuclear power plants cost more per kilowatt of installed capacity than conventional power plants do. Hence for the foreseeable future the capital costs of nuclear power plants will offset such advantages of nuclear fuel as cheapness and mobility.

The foregoing conclusions for both the developed and the underdeveloped countries rest on present-day expectations regarding the use of atomic energy. It is impossible to say whether or not the inherent promise of nuclear fuels – abundance, mobility, and economy – will begin to be realized within the forty-year time horizon of this analysis, but in the long run it seems almost certain that these intrinsic advantages will be captured in the technology developed to make use of atomic energy.

Minerals*

JULIAN W. FEISS

Deposits of important minerals that can be economically mined are poorly distributed over the surface of the earth. Modern substitutions may, however, alleviate some of this imbalance.

Although it is widely recognized that an industrial society requires a broad mineral-resource base, the extent to which modern production technology depends on mineral raw materials is seldom appreciated. It is easy to comprehend the needs for and the application of the traditional common metals: iron, copper, lead, tin, and the newer metal aluminium; but it is more difficult to comprehend the changes in technology that influence their quality, fabrication, and end use in world markets. The increased demand for new alloys requiring special additives, some of which a generation ago were hardly more than names in the periodic table, tremendously complicates the supply requirement. As a result the creation of an integrated minerals or metals industry, even where local mineral supplies exist, will greatly strain the technological resources of underdeveloped countries.

On the other hand, even countries without mineral wealth of their own should not find it too difficult to import the needed mineral supplies. The total estimated value of the world's mineral production in 1960 was approximately $50,000 million, of which fuels represented about $37,000 million. The value of all other minerals, including construction materials such as sand and gravel, came to only

*Valuable assistance in the preparation of this article was given by staff members of the U.S. Geological Survey and U.S. Bureau of Mines. Its publication has been authorized by the Director of the Geological Survey.

$13,000 million. Of this sum U.S. production for its own consumption and U.S. imports from other countries added up to approximately $7,000 million, leaving only about $6,000 million worth of non-fuel minerals to be consumed by the rest of the world. This translates into a world consumption, outside the United States, of only about $2 a head. In comparison, U.S. consumption in 1960 was roughly $40 a head. If allowance is made for a consumption of perhaps $10 to $30 a head in other well-developed countries, the per capita mineral consumption in the underdeveloped regions of the world is reduced to well below $1.

These figures can be viewed both optimistically and pessimistically. The pessimistic aspect is simply that more than two billion of the world's people consume non-fuel minerals at an annual rate measured in pennies and that if their consumption were ever to approach the consumption enjoyed in the more privileged countries, the drain on the world's mineral resources would be staggering. The optimistic aspect is that even those underdeveloped countries that are poor in minerals should be able to double and triple their present tiny rates of mineral consumption at a comparatively small cost in raw materials. This is in marked contrast to the prospect faced by fuel-poor countries in meeting their requirements, as described in 'Energy', by Sam H. Schurr, page 91. He estimates that in 1980 the underdeveloped countries of Asia, Africa, Latin America, and the Middle East will consume about 2.5 times more fuel than they did in 1960. If it is estimated that these countries spent $7,000 million for fuel in 1960, their 1980 bill, at current prices, will be more than $17,000 million. It is doubtful that the same countries consumed as much as $1,000 million worth of non-fuel minerals in 1960, so a comparable doubling or tripling of their consumption by 1980 would represent relatively little money.

Many of the underdeveloped nations of course count on exports of indigenous minerals to provide the foreign exchange needed for industrial development. Such countries can look forward to a steadily rising demand for ores and minerals from the United States and other well-developed countries of the world. The United States, for example, imports all its tin; more than 90 per cent of its manganese, antimony, beryllium, and chromium ores; more than 85 per cent of its nickel; about 75 per cent of its bauxite; and about 55 per cent of its zinc and lead. Across the board the United States consumes roughly 25 per cent of the world's total production of metals.

Estimates of metal consumption in the United States in 1975, made recently by the U.S. Bureau of Mines, project an increase of 50 to 65 per cent for zinc and copper, 135 per cent for lead, and more than 250 per cent for aluminium and tungsten. Originally the increase for steel was estimated at 80 per cent, but it was subsequently cut to 60 per cent.

The reduction in the steel estimate is noteworthy, because it reflects a basic shift in the pattern of metals use that has developed almost entirely since the end of World War II and has been accelerating. For years steel production was the great bellwether of the economy. What has happened, very simply, is that steel is losing its historic role as the symbol of economic potency. U.S. steel output reached a peak of 117 million tons in 1955, dropped below 100 million tons in 1958 and has stayed there since. As the chart on page 110 indicates, U.S. per capita consumption of steel in 1961 (488 kilograms) was exceeded by Sweden (544 kilograms), Czechoslovakia (493 kilograms), and West Germany (490 kilograms). In its revised projection for 1975 the Bureau of Mines is providing for a per capita increase in U.S. steel consumption of only about 10 per cent.

In the United States, probably more than in other countries, steel has run into increasing competition from aluminium, magnesium, titanium, structural concrete, and a variety of strong, tough plastics. Steel is also meeting competition from itself: common steels are being replaced by steel alloys that are stronger and do a given job with less weight. Last November the changing outlook for steel

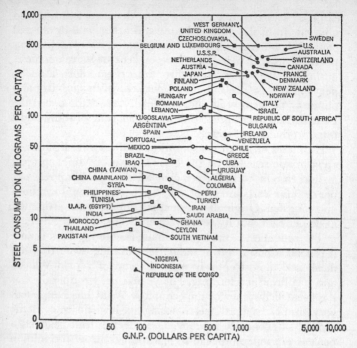

STEEL CONSUMPTION *v.* G.N.P. (Gross National Product), per capita, is shown for 1961. The chart is based on U.N. steel statistics and G.N.P. figures prepared largely by the Agency for International Development. For Communist countries G.N.P. is an estimate based on a report by the Centre for International Studies at the Massachusetts Institute of Technology. Sweden, Czechoslovakia, and West Germany now exceed the United States in per capita steel consumption. Symbols are as in the similar chart for energy use on page 94.

received documentation from an unexpected source. Speaking to an assemblage of economists and industrial managers in Moscow, Premier Khrushchev said: 'There was a time when the power of a state was measured in terms of the amount of steel it could produce. ... But now, when there are other materials competing with steel, such a criterion is no longer adequate.' He went on to say that some party officials 'have put on "steel blinkers" and now look and act as they were once taught. We now have a material that surpasses steel and costs less, and they still cry "Steel! Steel!"' Presumably he was referring to new plastics such as poly-ethylene and polypropylene. In any event, during the next twenty years the U.S.S.R. intends to expand plastics output twenty times and steel production only four times.

This is not to say, of course, that substantial steel capacity will not be needed in the emerging nations. Underdeveloped nations should, however, weigh various alternatives care-fully before each new addition to steel output. They prob-ably should not aspire to approach the West in per capita steel capacity.

A capsule history of changing materials technology can be found in the design of bridges. Early bridges were made of wood and stone. The first use of iron on a large scale began about a hundred and fifty years ago in bridges designed by Thomas Telford in England and Scotland. Steel remained almost unchallenged as a structural metal for bridges until the first all-aluminium bridge span was built over the Grass River at Massena, New York, in 1946. Four years later an all-aluminium highway bridge was completed across the Saguenay River at Arvida in the Canadian province of Quebec. The bridge contains a centre arch of 290-foot span that weighs only 200 tons – half the weight of an equivalent steel arch. Meanwhile European bridge builders have been reducing the amount of steel needed in bridges by using large members of pre-stressed concrete. These are concrete beams and slabs in which embedded steel cables or rods are held in tension.

The use of aluminium in bridges is symbolic of the grow-ing competition it offers to steel in construction jobs of many types. In 1961, for example, aluminium curtain walls were used for 18 per cent of the total wall area of non-residential buildings erected in the United States. Tens of thousands of tons of aluminium were also used in barges, truck trailers, railroad cars, and automobiles.

For underdeveloped countries an important role for aluminium is in replacing copper as a carrier of electric current. Even though aluminium is not so good a conductor as copper, its use can often be justified on other grounds. For example, in high-tension power lines aluminium, because it is lighter than copper, requires fewer supporting towers, with a consequent saving in steel. Asia is particularly deficient in copper ores but has at least 45 million tons of proved reserves of bauxite, the chief aluminium ore, and more can doubtless be found. As recently as 1960 only three Asian countries produced aluminium: China (both mainland and Taiwan), India, and Japan. Their total output, about 10 per cent of that of the United States and Canada combined, was not insignificant. Indonesia and the Philippines are now planning to build aluminium refineries. The principal obstacle to expanding production is finding adequate electric power.

The depletion of mineral resources, both in the United States and elsewhere, became a matter of serious concern immediately after World War II. Some pessimists felt that most of the world's high-grade ore deposits had already been discovered and that the minerals industry must be resigned to working ores of lower and lower grade. With the depletion of high-grade iron-ore deposits in the Lake Superior district, which has traditionally supplied more than 75 per cent of the U.S. total, steel companies began an intensive and costly programme to mine the lower-grade taconite and jaspilite ores, and to produce from them concentrated pellets suitable for the blast furnace. The cost of this programme to date has been more than $1,000 million, and in 1961 taconite and jaspilite pellets accounted for about 12 per cent of the iron in U.S. pig production.

But while the taconite programme was still in its early stages some of the world's largest high-grade deposits of iron were being found in Labrador, Ontario, Venezuela, Brazil,

Liberia, and other parts of West Africa. The iron-ore content of Cerro Bolívar in Venezuela has been placed at 500 million tons, or about 25 per cent of the ore thus far extracted and shipped directly from the great Mesabi Range of Minnesota. In the past few years another extensive deposit of iron ore has been found in the Hamersley Range of north-western Australia.

The result of all these new finds has been to raise the known world reserves of iron ore to more than 132,000 million tons of iron recoverable by present methods, a minimum increase of 60 per cent over estimated reserves in 1955. Nobody can say today which country has the biggest single reserve of iron ore, because economics and technology related to local factors determine whether material of a given grade is or is not ore. India has perhaps 21,000 million tons; Brazil may have even more; and Canada and West Africa are not far behind. The U.S.S.R. has recently disclosed that its iron-ore resources are slightly more than 30,000 million tons. It is clear, in short, that the world's total known resources of iron ore are many times greater than the world's possible needs through the year 2000.

The iron-ore discoveries in Ontario and Venezuela are outstanding instances of what has been achieved with new exploration techniques using air-borne instruments. These instruments include, in addition to the aerial camera, the air-borne magnetometer, the scintillometer, and electro-magnetic-induction devices. The air-borne magnetometer measures anomalies, or irregularities, in the earth's magnetic flux attributable to buried mineral deposits. The scintillometer measures the emanations from radio-active ores and is also widely used in oil prospecting because the radiation flux above oil pools is often less than that in the normal earth background. The electromagnetic-induction technique employs the principle used by wartime mine detectors.

The Marmora iron deposit in Ontario was first spotted by

air-borne magnetometer. Cerro Bolívar was identified as a promising site from inspection of aerial photographs and the presence of ore was confirmed by air-borne magnetometer. The big iron deposit of the Nimba Mountains in Liberia was located by air-borne magnetometer. And in the United States, which had already been prospected intensively for iron ore, the air-borne magnetometer has helped to locate large deposits on Pea Ridge in Missouri and near Morgantown, Pennsylvania.

The air-borne magnetometer can also indicate the possible location of minerals other than iron. The presence of non-magnetic ores, such as copper and bauxite, may be signalled by a magnetic reading that is below the normal background level. Thus the air-borne magnetometer was responsible for locating the New Hosko copper deposit in Quebec, a lead deposit in south-eastern Missouri, and large bauxite deposits in Surinam and Venezuela.

Electromagnetic surveying from the air has led to the discovery of a new copper deposit at Mattagami in Ontario and a huge new nickel deposit in Manitoba. The nickel deposit, known as the Thompson ore body, may be the most important find that has been made with the new air-borne geophysical methods.

Another new prospecting tool of growing importance is geochemistry. In this method sensitive chemical indicators are used to find traces of sought-for metals in soils, streams, and vegetation. These trace materials are then used as clues for locating a hidden ore body.

Air-borne geophysical methods are particularly well suited to underdeveloped regions where territories are large, ground surveying is difficult, and topographic maps are often non-existent. In the past ten years millions of square kilometres of Latin America, Africa, and Asia have been mapped photographically from the air and have been surveyed by one or more of the air-borne geophysical instruments. Although costs are high, they are orders of magnitude less than what it would cost to do the same job from

the ground. An air-borne survey combining the magnetometer and scintillometer costs about $7 per linear kilo-
metre, or about $6,000 per 1,000 square kilometres. If
electromagnetic induction is added, the total cost is $15,000
to $20,000 for the same area. Obviously it will take many
years and many millions of dollars to survey the world in
reasonable detail. Today only 65 per cent of the United
States has been topographically mapped and only 20 per
cent has been mapped geologically.

Even after an underdeveloped country (or a developed
one, for that matter) has discovered a deposit of ore worth
mining, the job has only begun. Unless the ore is exceptionally rich, accessible, and convenient to transportation, a
heavy capital investment is usually required to dig it out,
process it, and move it to market. Usually technical and
financial assistance from one of the developed nations will
have to be sought. And gauging the proper capital investment may be difficult. It is often a mistake, for example,
to mechanize a mine in an underdeveloped land as fully as
a comparable mine in a more advanced nation. Frequently
the capital needed for high mechanization could be better
spent elsewhere in the economy. Since most underdeveloped
lands have a labour surplus it may be better to employ many
workers at a modest wage than to employ a few skilled machine operators at a wage disproportionate to that prevailing in other fields.

Another difficult question is whether to sell the crude ore
as it is mined or to beneficiate it and thereby obtain a higher
market price and lower freight rates. Again, the cost of a
beneficiation plant must be weighed against other demands
for capital. Whatever the decision, a poor country lucky
enough to find a sizeable ore deposit must recognize that it
has found an important capital asset. To hoard it and leave
it unmined would be folly. Last spring at Geneva, Harrison
S. Brown, of the California Institute of Technology, spoke
on this point at the United Nations Conference on the
Application of Science and Technology for the Benefit of the

Less Developed Areas. Funds derived from the sale of mineral resources, Brown said,

should be converted to other forms of capital that are of equal or greater value, particularly into basic industrial installations and into power, transportation, and communication systems. The conversion of high-grade resource assets into current living expenses by means of export can lead to tragedy.

If an underdeveloped country wishes to convert a portion of its ore into finished metal, it faces another level of capital cost and technological difficulty. Refining requires supplementary materials, which may or may not be readily available. For example, iron production requires limestone and metallurgical coal that can be converted to coke. Throughout most of Africa, Latin America, and Asia such coal is scarce. In fact, it can be set down as a rule that no nation has yet built an advanced economy without a cheap and ready supply of metallurgical coal.

The problem of producing iron without high-grade coal is one to which the Western world, with all its vaunted technology, cannot supply a ready-made solution. The problem is being worked on, however, and a number of processes look promising. There are two general approaches. One is to convert low-rank coals into a coke with the properties needed in a blast furnace. The other is to reduce the iron ore directly with low-rank coal, oil, or natural gas by a technique not requiring a blast furnace.

The F.M.C. Corporation and the United States Steel Corporation have jointly developed a process that converts low-rank coals to blast-furnace coke. In this process the coal is crushed and partially oxidized in a 'fluidized bed': a reaction chamber in which fine particles behave somewhat like a fluid. After moisture and volatile hydrocarbons have been driven off, the particles are pressed into briquettes, which are further treated to yield a product with properties almost identical with those of blast-furnace coke.

A number of direct-reduction processes bypassing the blast furnace have been studied. One of them, called the

Strategic-Udy process, is being tried on a pilot-plant scale at the Orinoco Steel Plant of Corporación Venezolana de Guayana (C.V.G.). The process, conceived by Marvin Udy, had been developed jointly by the Strategic Metals Corporation and the Koppers Company, Inc. In the process low-rank Venezuelan coal, iron ore, and fluxing materials are fed into a giant rotary kiln, where partial reduction of the iron ore takes place. The kiln product is transferred directly to an electric furnace, which completes the reduction and produces pig iron.

This chapter has mentioned only a few of the minerals essential to a vigorous economy. Of the sixty-five metallic elements in the periodic table the United States uses thirty in substantial commercial quantities. It uses ten of them in amounts exceeding 50,000 tons a year and another ten or twelve in amounts exceeding 1,000 tons a year. Only one of them, magnesium, which is extracted from sea water and other brines, is in virtually unlimited supply. In addition to metals the United States consumes more than twenty other mineral substances (for example, salts of various kinds, sulphur, bromine, chlorine, iodine, phosphate rock, asbestos, gypsum, talc, and mica) in quantities exceeding 1,000 tons a year. Of these perhaps half are quite abundant and create few problems either for the United States or for most under-developed countries.

In spite of the accelerating drain on the world's mineral resources it is now becoming recognized that they will never really be exhausted. Just as advances in technology have made it possible to exploit today ores so lean they would have been considered worthless only fifty years ago, new advances will make it possible to extract metals from still leaner ores in the future. In effect, technology keeps creating new resources. Meanwhile new geophysical and geo-chemical tools have uncovered a remarkable number of unexpectedly rich mineral deposits, which the world, if it is wise, can use as capital assets to advance the well-being of all.

Education for Development

FREDERICK HARBISON

Capital investments can be made not only in industry but also in people – a comparison of the problems of education in four underdeveloped countries: Nyasaland, Colombia, China, and Egypt.

The progress of a nation depends first and foremost on the progress of its people. Unless it develops their spirit and human potentialities it cannot develop much else – materially, economically, politically, or culturally. The basic problem of most of the underdeveloped countries is not a poverty of natural resources but the underdevelopment of their human resources. Hence their first task must be to build up their human capital – in more human terms, to improve the education, skills, and hopefulness, and thus the mental and physical health, of their men, women, and children.

The way to start seems obvious and quite uncomplicated: build schools and launch a massive programme of primary and secondary education and technical training. But the problem is not really that simple. These countries are not in a position to adopt any such crash programme. Their limited funds for investment in education must be placed where they will do the most good. Moreover, the shotgun approach may create more difficulties than it solves; in some countries the training of more engineers, for example, may produce nothing but trouble. In any country, developed or underdeveloped, education can become socially malignant if its people do not have a chance and the incentives to use it.

Each country therefore needs to think out a strategy for the education and development of its human resources. The strategy should be based on the character and traditions of its people, the stage of the country's development, and the opportunities available for its advancement. This conclusion has been strongly impressed on me by a comprehensive study of seventy-five countries I have made in collaboration with Charles A. Myers, of the Massachusetts Institute of Technology, published as a book under the title *Education, Manpower and Economic Growth*.

I shall present in this chapter some of the main ideas that have come out of the study, illustrating them with brief descriptions of the situations in four countries that represent different stages of development, with problems typical of each stage. The four countries are Nyasaland, Colombia, China, and Egypt.

Nyasaland is a small country in east central Africa, fairly representative of a number of the newly emerging African states (Tanganyika, Kenya, Nigeria, Mali, Gabon, Northern Rhodesia). It ranks as one of the least developed countries. It has been exploited for three cash crops – tea, tobacco, and cotton – grown on large plantations that until now were owned and managed mainly by white settlers. Most of the country's three million people are small farmers scratching out a meagre living; the estimated per capita income is only about $60 a year. Modern industrialization is far beyond the present reach of the country and its economic growth must therefore depend largely on the development of its agriculture.

Nyasaland now has its own government and legislature, but it still must depend on foreigners to fill about 90 per cent of the high-level jobs in government and private occupations that require people with at least a secondary-school education. In the entire country there are only a handful of native doctors, one lawyer, one engineer, and not a single native stenographer. The country has no scientists of its own. Not more than about four hundred Nyasas have completed secondary school and only about fifty have had any university education – all, of course, outside the country.

Although about 40 per cent of the children of elementary

school age attend school, the drop-out rate is very high: of 33,000 who started school in 1951, only 620 went as far as ten years of schooling. Most of the country's elementary school teachers are unqualified, having had no more than a primary education themselves, and in the secondary schools only about a third of the qualified teachers are African.

Naturally the Nyasaland government has an acute desire to make the country truly independent by training Africans for the high-level jobs in government, business, and education that now have to be turned over to non-Africans. Since this will be at best a slow process, it appears to be the better part of discretion for the government to keep the foreigners as long as possible and enlist their cooperation in training their eventual replacements. And in the replacement programme the government's best prospect is to upgrade and train Africans on the job – within the government, business establishments, plantations, schools, and other institutions in which it needs skilled people.

The Nyasas who take over these jobs naturally want to be paid the same salaries as the foreigners they replace. The government finds it difficult to match the salaries, as it faces extraordinarily high expenses for the educational and other new services it must organize. Yet it must establish a rational system of incentives for its own people, making compensation commensurate with the importance of the job rather than with family status, political connexions, or other considerations that have dictated payment in the past. Without a proper system of incentives for ability and performance, the investment in education will be wasted from the standpoint of contributing to the country's progress.

In building its educational system for the next two decades Nyasaland faces some hard choices. How much should it invest in elementary education and how much in secondary? If it is to make headway as a nation, it needs a literate people and a stronger wellspring of schooled youngsters coming up to build its future. On the other hand, it must have as soon as possible a core of educated Nyasas who can serve as the leaders of its economic and political development when the foreigners leave. Necessarily, then, for the next ten years it should give the highest priority to secondary-school education, which today enrolls only 1.5 per cent of Nyasaland's children of high school age.

Should it concentrate on general education in the secondary schools or on vocational and technical training? Again the decision is difficult but unavoidable: general education is clearly indicated. Vocational training is four to five times more expensive per student; there are no schoolteachers competent to give it; it is difficult to forecast exactly what vocational skills the new nation will need most; and such training can be given more efficiently on the job.

In the case of higher education the choice is also tricky but, for good and understandable reasons, it is less difficult. For some time to come it would be cheaper for Nyasaland to send students to universities abroad and pay their tuition than to build a university. For national prestige, however, and to retain its ablest youths instead of running the danger of losing them permanently, it is important to Nyasaland to have its own university. Consequently the present government has committed itself to building an institution of higher education. It will be able to focus on the kinds of higher learning the nation needs most and to stand as a symbol and leader of its culture.

Although for the next decade elementary schooling must take a back seat in financing, it need not languish. The main emphasis there should be on improving the quality of teaching and seeing to it that those pupils who do enter school go through to the end of the primary grades. A beginning can also be made in introducing modern tools of education, such as appropriate local textbooks and study materials, visual aids, radio, television, and other devices. And once the immediate necessities of secondary and higher education are taken care of, Nyasaland should move on to provide elementary schooling for all its children.

Last but not least, Nyasaland and all other countries in its situation have a great need and opportunity for adult education. Formal classes in basic education for the country's men and women could go a long way towards making up for the deficiencies of their early schooling and raising the national literacy. In addition, the adult education programme should offer extension courses in agriculture, health, child care, home building, and other subjects that will be an immediate contribution to the improvement of the lives of the people.

Colombia, usually classed as an underdeveloped country, is fairly well advanced compared with Nyasaland. On our scale of measurement of human resources it stands about midway between primitive Nyasaland and the developed countries of western Europe. We classify it as a 'partly developed' country, along with some other countries in Latin America and nations such as Turkey, Iran, Pakistan, and Ghana.

Colombia has 13.6 per cent of its children of high school age enrolled in secondary schools, compared with 1.5 per cent in Nyasaland; it has twenty-five universities, with 1.8 per cent of its college-age population enrolled; its gross national product per capita is about $260, against Nyasaland's $60. Colombia is still primarily agricultural, with 54 per cent of its people engaged in farming, but it has rapidly growing industries and its economic growth in the near future will depend mainly on further industrialization.

For top-level jobs Colombia has all the educated manpower it needs, except in engineering and science. But it is very short of skilled people at the technical and sub-professional levels: technicians, foremen, assistants in agricultural research and guidance, teachers, nurses, and so on.

Colombia's system of higher education is unbalanced, offering as it does many courses of study in the humanities and law but few in science and engineering. Moreover, the quality of its universities is low: they are poorly equipped with libraries and laboratories and rely almost entirely on

ill-trained, part-time teachers. The emphasis on the humanities and law at the expense of the sciences is an expression of
the sacrifice of quality for quantity; it costs only about a
sixth to a fourth as much to give the students law courses as
it does to teach them engineering or science. Thus Colombia
finds (as countries starting their own universities also do)
that it can accommodate the largest number of students per
dollar by skimping on science and technology.

Even more inadequate is the training of technicians and
sub-professional workers. Compared with 23,000 students in
the universities, Colombia in 1962 had only 1,150 in technical institutes; it is turning out more engineers than technicians, although the proportion should be the other way
around. In the developing countries even more markedly
than in advanced ones, young people prefer college to a
technical school by a wide margin because it means higher
prestige and better pay when they graduate.

Oddly enough, although Colombia supports twenty-five
universities and offers a university education at a very low
tuition, it shows much less interest in secondary education.
There are few public secondary schools; most Colombians
who want to go to college must prepare at a private school.
Enrolments in the private preparatory schools are limited,
and less than 5 per cent of Colombian families can afford
the fees. Thus secondary education in Colombia is a bottle-
neck, allowing the children of the rich to go on to universities, instead of being a door leading to opportunity for the
development of the country's able youth.

Colombia's primary schooling also is underdeveloped.
Considerable money has been spent in building schools, but
the curriculum is poorly planned, the teaching substandard,
and the drop-out rate high. By the third grade a majority of
the pupils have quit, and only about an eighth of the children who enter the first grade go all the way through the
five years of elementary school.

The strongest element in Colombia's educational system
is a programme of training factory workers, financed by a

tax on employers and controlled by their organizations. Outstanding is the work of the National Service of Apprenticeship (S.E.N.A.). It has built and equipped modern vocational training centres, employs expert instructors, and not only trains apprentices but also gives in-service instruction of many kinds to workers in the factories.

In Colombia as in Nyasaland the greatest immediate need, from the standpoint of developing the country's human resources, is to expand and reform the secondary school system. Along with providing free secondary education for all those who are qualified to take advantage of it, Colombia should develop the agricultural, scientific, and engineering faculties of its universities. It should improve the quality of the student body and of the teaching in the universities rather than merely enrol as many students as possible. This shift in emphasis would be politically unpopular, but a proper system of incentive could make it palatable. The government will need to take the lead in improving the relative pay and status of scientists, engineers, and workers in other professions where there are critical shortages. The same strategy should be applied to the recruitment of people into the technical and sub-professional occupations. These jobs probably could be made sufficiently inviting if the pay were comparable to that received by general college graduates and if the sub-professionals were given opportunities for promotion to professional posts by taking spare-time university courses.

China, our third illustration, also is a partly developed country. Its educational enrolment ratios are much like Colombia's: it enrols about 40 per cent of the population in elementary schools, 14 per cent in secondary schools, and 1 per cent in higher education. But there the resemblance ends. The mere statistics in this case give little indication of the size and intensity of China's educational effort and progress.

The Communist government of mainland China has organized an all-out programme to train and mobilize manpower. In the nine years between 1950 and 1959 China increased its enrolment in elementary schools threefold, in secondary schools ninefold, and in higher education sixfold. Today the country has 100 million students in school – more than the combined totals of the United States and the U.S.S.R. It is turning out three fourths as many engineers as the United States and ranks third in the world in this respect, after the U.S.S.R. and the United States, in that order. Perhaps the most remarkable statistic, giving the measure of China's effort, is that, of the country's present 250,000 scientists and engineers, 90 per cent have been trained since the Communist government came to power in 1949.

Once a land of philosophers, artists, and peasants, China is being transformed into a nation of technocrats. Its Confucian sages have been replaced by scientists, engineers, and industrial managers. Its educational programme is geared mainly to industrialization. In its universities the humanities have been downgraded, and more than 55 per cent of the students are enrolled in science and technology, compared with 25 per cent in most other countries. China seeks to gain standing as a world power through rapid industrialization, and as its first objective it aims to reach, by 1967, Britain's level in industrial production.

China has a long way to go economically. Its gross national product per capita is probably no more than $75. The strategy of its officials and planners in education seems to be to try to do everything at once – to attack all the expedient approaches and above all to emphasize action. As recently described by a Chinese Communist newspaper, the educational programme includes schools operated not only by the state but also by all kinds of agencies, including factories, mines, and 'street organizations'. The Chinese people are studying full time and part time, in school and at home, in tuition courses and free ones. The quality of most of their education, including much of that in the universities, is questionable, and so is the strategy of an onward rush by any and every possible means. It may result in crippling steps backward as well as leaps ahead.

Egypt, our fourth example, is an odd case: except in certain specialities, it has a larger number of highly skilled people than it can use. The reason I have chosen to discuss its situation is that Egypt represents certain countries (among them India) that seem to be spending more effort in producing high-level skills than is justified by their present stage of development.

By most criteria Egypt is an underdeveloped country – limited in resources, mainly a nation of farmers (65 per cent), low in gross national product per capita ($140), and only semi-literate in terms of the proportion of its children who go to elementary school. But taking secondary and higher education into account, Egypt is a semi-advanced country.

In proportion to its population Egypt has more students in universities than Britain and twice as many in secondary and higher education as West Germany. Egypt has an alarmingly high rate of unemployment among university graduates, and the government is hard pressed to find jobs for them as junior clerks and minor functionaries in the already overstaffed ministries. Thousands of Egyptian schoolteachers, engineers, and agronomists have left home to teach and work in neighbouring Arab countries.

The government of Gamal Abdel Nasser is attempting to relieve the pressure of high-level unemployment and correct Egypt's unbalanced educational system in several ways. It is encouraging its unemployed graduates to work in less developed countries and is inviting those countries to send students to its universities. It plans to expand and improve the education of skilled technicians and administrative personnel, of whom it has a shortage. It could and should proceed rapidly to provide elementary schooling for all its children, for which it can easily train all the teachers it needs. Common sense also suggests that Egypt should cut back its university enrolments and raise the standards of secondary and higher education. The clamour of parents and their children for more education, however, makes this politically impossible. Consequently it appears that Egypt's best hope is to go in for kinds of economic development that give maximum opportunities for the employment of highly educated people.

These four countries – Nyasaland, Colombia, China, and Egypt – are merely samples of the seventy-five that Myers and I have studied, from the world's most underdeveloped nations to the most advanced. I should like to sum up a few of the generalizations that emerged from the study.

First, there is a strong correlation between a country's educational development and its economic productivity. Using an indicator of educational development based on the enrolment in secondary schools and universities, we found that in the seventy-five countries the coefficient of correlation between educational level and the gross national product per capita is 0.888. The best single indicator of a country's wealth in human resources is the proportion of its young people enrolled in secondary schools.

Second, education alone is not enough to assure a nation's prosperity. For example, in its level of education Japan certainly ranks among the world's top ten countries, but its gross national product per capita is only about $300 – far below the advanced countries' $1,100 average. Egypt, India, and Thailand also rank high in education and relatively low in gross national product per capita, whereas in countries such as Saudi Arabia, Liberia, and Venezuela the situation is reversed. Obviously many factors other than education enter into a country's economic progress, including its natural resources, foreign markets, outside assistance, and so on. Therefore we cannot say that an investment of x dollars in education will produce a y result in economic growth. All we can predict is that a well-educated and motivated people will do extraordinarily well, as the little country of Israel, with its very limited natural resources, is demonstrating today.

Third, in its educational investment a country must

adopt a balanced programme suited to its own needs and stage of development, or it may run into trouble. It will have a number of choices to make, and for its educational programme it will have to find the best compromise among: (1) quality and quantity, (2) science and the humanities, (3) vocational training in school and on the job, (4) regulation of salary incentives by the state and by the market, and (5) the needs of the individual and the needs of the state.

Fourth, a country's educational investment and goals must be shaped realistically to the level of its economic development. Whereas in a nation such as the United States a high school education barely qualifies a person for a semiskilled job, in an underdeveloped or partly developed country it may suffice for the higher positions, until the country is able to advance to a higher level.

Fifth, education generates a strong demand and push for more education. This has been true in all the advancing countries. The development of elementary schools creates a demand for secondary education and this in turn for higher education of many kinds. Unlike the demand for material goods, which may become saturated, the demand for education is never really satisfied, not only because it offers the individual an endless frontier of advancement in career and status but also because it opens irresistible frontiers for the human mind and curiosity.

Detailed quantitative research on education as a factor in national development is itself in need of development. Many of the variables can be identified as precisely as variables in economics, and it should be possible to work out rational strategies in educational policy, as in other economic affairs.

Unfortunately it seems most unlikely that science will ever find a formula for the abolition of inertia and political immorality. But education contains seeds that, as history has repeatedly shown, can inspire and energize a whole people.

The Structure of Development

WASSILY LEONTIEF

Analysis of an economy by the 'input-output' method reveals its internal structure, which is dictated largely by technology. Applied to underdeveloped economies, the technique maps out paths to growth.

Estimates of gross national product, total consumption, income per capita, rate of investment, and similar indices of economic activity are now compiled and published by practically all countries. Such figures give quantitative expression to the otherwise plainly apparent fact that some countries are rich and others poor. When these figures have been plotted over the recent past, they indicate that the gap between the rich and the poor has been widening. These statistics do not of themselves suggest any ready explanation of the difference in over-all performance among the national economies. Nor do they point to any practical ways to narrow the gap.

The earth's resources are ample for the needs of the present world population and even for a much larger one. It is true that the distribution of resources is uneven. It is also true that the poor countries do not make full use of the resources they have. They raise less food per acre and per man-hour, and they realize little of the value of their mineral wealth above the price of the ore or the crude oil at the dockside. Described in these terms the disparities in the well-being of nations are nowadays summed up in the somewhat more useful observation that they reflect differences in degree of development.

For the understanding that must precede any constructive action it is necessary to penetrate below the surface of global statistics and such round terms as 'development'. Each economic system – even that of an underdeveloped country

– has a complicated internal structure. Its performance is determined by the mutual relations of its differentiated component parts, just as the motion of the hands of a clock is governed by the gears inside. Over the past twenty-five years the internal economic gearwork of a large number of countries has been described with increasing clarity and precision by a technique known as 'inter-industry analysis', or 'input-output analysis'. Because the results improve as more fine-grained statistics are fed into it, the technique has demonstrated its effectiveness largely in the study of more highly developed economic systems.

The data of input-output analysis are the flows of goods and services inside the economy that underlie the summary statistics by which economic activity is conventionally measured. Displayed in the input-output table, the pattern of transactions between industries and other major sectors of the system shows that the more developed the economy, the more its internal structure resembles that of other developed economies. Moreover, from one economy to the next the ratios between these internal transactions and the external total activity of the system – true gear ratios in the sense that they are determined largely by technology – turn out to be relatively constant.

Recent advances in input-output analysis and in the bookkeeping of underdeveloped countries have made it possible to apply the technique to a number of these economies. Their input-output tables show that in addition to being smaller and poorer they have internal structures that are different, because they are incomplete, compared with the developed economies. From such comparative studies a fundamental analytical approach to the structure of economic development is now emerging.

Construction of a national input-output table is a major statistical enterprise. By now tables for some forty countries have been prepared. Some countries (among the underdeveloped countries: Israel, Egypt, Spain, and Argentina) have published comprehensive, detailed, and quite accurate tables. Others, having just entered the field, have not yet advanced beyond rather sketchy compilations of limited accuracy. The growing literature in this field, however, testifies to the fact that, with the practical know-how gained in the preparation of the first experimental table, the second- and third-generation tables become invested with the elaboration and professional finish required for an effective scientific instrument.

INPUT

OUTPUT	SECTOR 1: AGRICULTURE	SECTOR 2: MANUFACTURES	FINAL DEMAND	TOTAL OUTPUT
SECTOR 1: AGRICULTURE	25	20	55	100 UNITS
SECTOR 2: MANUFACTURES	14	6	30	50 UNITS
HOUSEHOLD SERVICES	80	180	40	300 UNITS

INPUT/OUTPUT COEFFICIENTS

	SECTOR 1: AGRICULTURE	SECTOR 2: MANUFACTURES	FINAL DEMAND
SECTOR 1: AGRICULTURE	0.25	0.40	0.183
SECTOR 2: MANUFACTURES	0.14	0.12	0.100
HOUSEHOLD SERVICES	0.80	3.60	0.133

INPUT-OUTPUT table (*top*) and input-coefficient matrix (*bottom*) show 'internal' transactions between productive sectors of a simple model economy in relation to the 'Final demand' and 'Total output' of each sector. The table displays outputs from each sector in a corresponding horizontal row, inputs to each sector in a vertical column. In the matrix the columns display the ratio between each input to a sector and the total output of the sector (see text on page 132).

The input-output table is not merely a device for displaying or storing information; it is above all an analytical tool. Depending on the purpose at hand and the availaability of reliable information, the economy can be broken down into any number of industries or sectors. The table for the U.S. economy as of 1947, prepared by the Bureau of Labor Statistics of the U.S. Department of Labor, has 450 sectors. For purposes of this demonstration an economy can be broken down into two industrial sectors: agriculture and manufactures (see page 131). In the table for such a simple model economy the numbers in the horizontal row labelled 'Agriculture' show that this sector, in the course of delivering 55 units of output and end products to 'Final demand' and 20 units as raw materials (for example, cotton) to 'Manufactures', delivers 25 units of its own output (for example, feed grains) to itself. 'Final demand' can here be taken as including the goods and services consigned to investment and export as well as to current consumption in the households of the economy. The total output of 100 units from the agricultural sector therefore satisfies both the 'direct' final demand for its end products and the 'indirect' demand for its intermediate products. On the input side the numbers in the column labelled 'Agriculture' show that in order to produce 100 units of total output this sector absorbs not only 25 units of its own product but also 14 units of input (for example, implements) from 'Manufactures' and 80 units – of labour, capital, and other prime factors – from the sector called, by convention, 'Household services'.

The great value of input-output analysis is that it surfaces the indirect internal transactions of an economic system and brings them into the reckonings of economic theory. Within each sector there is a relatively invariable connexion between the inputs it draws from other sectors and its contribution to the total output of the economy. This holds for an underdeveloped economy, where the input from 'Household services' necessary to produce 100 units of agricultural

INTERNAL STRUCTURES of model economies are revealed by input-output tables. Black squares signify inputs from a sector in a given horizontal row to sectors in the vertical columns intersected by the row; open triangles, the input from each sector to 'Final demand' (D); black triangles, the total output (T) of each sector; open squares, the inputs of prime factors from 'Household services' (H). The table at upper left shows a completely 'interdependent' economy; the table at upper right shows a random pattern of inter-industry transactions. The latter table appears at lower left with sectors rearranged (note the sequence of sector 'call numbers'); this 'triangulation' of the table reveals the hierarchical pattern of inter-industry transactions. The 'block triangular' model at lower right shows the interdependence of industries within blocks, as in the first model, and hierarchical relation between blocks as in the third (see pages 135–6).

output might represent a full eighty man-years of labour, as well as for a highly developed country where this input would reflect a larger component of capital and is likely to be offset by inputs of fertilizers, insecticides, and the like, from the industrial sectors. In fact, for use as an analytical tool, the input-output table must be recast into a matrix showing the input ratios, or coefficients, characteristic of each sector. The input-output table for the model economy, re-cast into such a matrix, shows that 0.25 unit of agricultural output, 0.14 unit of manufactures, and 0.8 unit of prime factors from 'Household services' are required to produce one unit of total output from the agricultural sector (see illustration on page 131).

Each sector or industry thus has its own 'cooking recipe'. The recipe is determined in the main by technology; in a real economy it changes slowly over the periods of time usually involved in economic forecasting and planning. The input-coefficient matrix can be derived, as it is in the present demonstration, from the inter-industry transaction for a given year, from engineering data, or from a combination of these and other sources of information. For any bill of final demand, the matrix makes it possible to compute the inputs each industry must absorb from all other industries in the course of fulfilling the final demand for its output and meeting the indirect demand for that output generated by the final demands of the industries to which it in turn supplies inputs. The computation involves the iterative solution of a set of simultaneous linear equations. Since the number of equations increases as the square of the number of sectors, the computing of a table sufficiently detailed to yield significant information is a task for machines.

It was the labour of computation that prompted the first systematic studies of the structural characteristics of an economy as they are displayed in an input-output table. During the late 1940s Marshall K. Wood, George D. Dantzig, and their associates in Project Scoop of the U.S. Air Force undertook to rearrange the rows and columns in a table of the

U.S. economy in such a way as to minimize the computation required to yield numerical solutions. Such rearrangement brought into sharper relief the inter-industry and inter-sectoral transactions that tie industries and sectors together in the subunits of the total structure of the economy. As more and more countries have begun to compile tables, comparative studies of their structural characteristics have begun to appear.

Dependence and independence, hierarchy and circularity (or multiregional interdependence) are the four basic concepts of structural analysis. The definition and practical significance of each of these ideas can be demonstrated visually by schematic model tables in which black squares rather than numbers signify the presence or absence of inter-industry transactions (see illustration on page 133). In the first of these tables a square appears in every one of the 225 boxes formed by the intersection of the 15 numbered rows and columns of the industrial sectors. Each industry in such a system is dependent on all the others; it supplies inputs to all other sectors and draws inputs from all of them. Translated into mathematical language, this means that each of the 15 variables representing the output of each of the sectors figures directly in each of the input-output equations. In the operation of this economy any increase in the output delivered by any one sector to final demand (represented by the open triangle at the right-hand end of the row) would require an increase in the inputs to this sector (reading down the column) from all other sectors without exception. Hence a single increase in direct demand can set up a whole chain of indirect demands, ultimately increasing the total output of every sector in the system.

A more likely and natural system is represented by the model in which some boxes are empty. The industry in whose column one of these empty boxes appears draws no input (or perhaps an insignificant input) from the industry whose row it intersects at this point. If the corresponding box formed by the reverse combination of column and row is empty, then these two sectors can be described as being independent of each other. Where inter-sectoral dependence is indicated by a square in this table, however, one such square may trigger a whole chain of indirect demands, finally involving both members of an apparently independent pair of sectors.

Such relations become clearer in the model in which all the squares fall below the diagonal running from the upper left corner to the lower right corner of the matrix. Actually this 'triangular' system was constructed by rearrangement of the rows and columns of the 'natural' system described in the preceding paragraph, as is indicated by the sequence in which the call numbers of the sectors now appear. The highly structural hierarchical relation between the different sectors was obscured in the first random display – an accidental effect, perhaps, of the sequence in which the census bureau of this imaginary economy assigned call numbers to the sectors. In the rearranged table it can be plainly seen that sector 9, now in the far left column, absorbs inputs from all the other sectors but delivers its entire output directly to final demand. Sector 8, now in the far right column, requires for its operation, in addition to a portion of its own output, only labour, capital, and other prime factors from 'Household services'; on the other hand, this sector delivers inputs to all other sectors as well as to final demand.

In the hierarchical order of an economy with a strictly triangular matrix, the sectors above and below the horizontal row of any given sector bear quite different relations to that sector. Those below are its suppliers; any increase in final demand for its product generates indirect demands that cascade down the diagonal slope of the matrix and leave the sectors above unaffected. The sectors above, however, are its customers; an increase in final demand for the output of any one of them generates indirect demand for the output of the sector in question. An economist charged with the task of computing the indirect effects of an increase in final demand for the output of this sector would need to know, therefore, only the input coefficients for sectors below it. If he wants to compute the indirect effects on this sector of demand originating elsewhere, he needs to work only with the input coefficients for this sector and the sectors above it. In the case of the fourth 'block triangular' model he would find that relations between sectors within each block are similar to the mutual interdependence that ties together all the sectors in the first of these model systems, whereas the relations between the blocks ('multiregional interdependence') are analogous to those between the sectors in the triangular model.

The convenience of the economist and the computing machine does not, of course, constitute the sole or the most significant purpose served by such rearrangement of an input-output table. The 'triangulation' of the table serves also to expose the internal structure of the inter-industry transactions. These define groups and blocks of more closely related industries. The forecaster is likely to find that he must reckon with the fortunes of all the industries within a group in order to plot the future course of one of them. The planner may discover that the effort to promote the growth of an industry in one block requires the prior development of industries in another block and may trigger the development of industries in still another block.

The triangulation of a real input-output table – that is, the discovery of its peculiar structural properties – is a challenging task. It is complicated by the fact that one must take into account not only the distinction between zero and non-zero entries but also the often more important difference between their actual numerical magnitudes. The degree to which triangulation reveals significant structural details depends also on the fineness of the sectoral breakdown. A single entry in a highly aggregated table may conceal the solid block of a triangular matrix or a narrow strip of finer inter-sectoral relations. Lack of sufficiently detailed information about the internal structure of groups and blocks of industries may impose severe limitations on attempts to explain the behaviour of the economic system as a whole.

The larger and the more advanced an economy is, the more complete and articulated is its structure. The United States and western Europe respectively produce about a third and a quarter of the world's total output of goods and services. It is not surprising, therefore, to discover that their input-output tables yield the same triangulation. Discounting the larger over-all size of the U.S. economy, the similarity between the two sets of inter-sectoral relations comes vividly to the fore when the triangulated input-output tables of the two systems are superposed on each other (see illustration on pull-out). Between them they contain – with some well-known but minor exceptions – a complete array of economic activities of all possible kinds.

Each of the industries in this combined table has its own peculiar input requirements, characteristic of that industry not only in the United States and in Europe but also wherever it happens to be in operation. The recipes for satisfying the appetite of a blast furnace, a cement kiln, or a thermo-electric power station will be the same in India or Peru as it is, say, in Italy or California. In a sense the input-coefficient matrix derived from the U.S.–western Europe input-output table represents a complete cook-book of modern technology. It constitutes, without doubt, the structure of a fully developed economy in so far as development has proceeded anywhere today.

An underdeveloped economy can now be defined as underdeveloped to the extent that it lacks the working parts of this system. This lack can be explained in narrowly economic terms as due to the amount and distribution of productively invested capital; in social terms, as a reflection of the composition and efficiency of the labour force; or in geographical terms, as the result of the country's endowment with natural resources. This last element deserves special mention, because much has been said in recent years about the possibility of designing custom-made technologies to meet the special conditions prevailing in certain underdeveloped countries. Celso Furtado, in the chapter 'The Development of Brazil' (see page 180), mentions the scarcity of coal in that country and speaks of the need for a new technology to reduce the iron in the abundant local ores. Leaving aside the intrinsic merit of such proposals, the fact is that the choice of alternative technologies hardly exists. The process of development consists essentially in the installation and building of an approximation of the system embodied in the advanced economies of the United States and western Europe and, more recently, of the U.S.S.R. – with due allowance for limitations imposed by the local mix of resources and the availability of technology to exploit them.

In the absence of such complete development a country can consume goods without producing them because it can import them. It must pay for its imports, however, by producing other goods for export instead of for domestic consumption. Two countries can thus display identical, or at least very similar, patterns of domestic final demand and yet have very different patterns of production. The smaller and the less developed a country is, the more it can be expected to exploit its productive capacity independently of its immediate needs and to bridge the gap between production and consumption by means of foreign trade. Consequently the full diagnosis of the ills of an underdeveloped country – as well as the formulation of a realistic development plan – requires a detailed quantitative analysis of the dependence of all the domestic industries not only on the configuration of final demand but also on the composition of the country's foreign trade.

Of all the developing countries, Israel possesses the most detailed and complete statistics necessary for an analysis of this kind. An input-output table prepared from data compiled by Michael Bruno of the Bank of Israel and triangulated according to the U.S.-Europe plan appears on the pull-out. In this table final demand is broken down into three components: domestic final demand (including investment as well as consumption), exports, and imports. The import figures, printed in italics, are negative figures with respect to the country's foreign-trade account and must be subtracted from the sum total of domestic final demand, exports, and the deliveries of the commodity in question to other industrial sectors (indirect demand) in order to arrive at the figures for total output at the end of each row.

Israel's heavy dependence on imports becomes apparent on inspection of the table. In five sectors ('Ships, aircraft', 'Machinery', 'Basic metals', 'Industrial crops', and 'Mining') it can be seen that the country's imports exceed domestic output by large margins. In five other sectors ('Grains, fodder', 'Forestry', 'Motor vehicles', 'Electrical appliances', and 'Paper and products') imports are equal to more than 50 per cent of domestic production. Imports exceed domestic final demand plus exports in six sectors. ('Grains, fodder', 'Basic metals', 'Paper and products', 'Basic chemicals', 'Industrial crops', and 'Mining'); this is because the indirect demand for imports of the commodities in question exceeds final demand. Most of these imports, in other words, are distributed as inputs to other industries along the row in which they are entered.

Perhaps the most useful way to see how Israel – or any other underdeveloped country – stands today is to construct a model of the economy as it would appear if it enjoyed self-sufficiency; that is, to determine the structure of production Israel would have to achieve in order to maintain its present actual consumption and investment entirely from domestic output and without recourse to foreign trade. Such a model will show, among other things, how far Israel falls short of possessing a fully articulated modern industrial economy, in which sectors it is weakest, and in which sectors it can push its development most fruitfully.

The first step in the construction of such a model is to prefabricate the sector 'modules' from which it is to be built. This means to compute from the input-coefficient matrix of the economy the inputs that are required – directly and in-directly – to enable each sector to deliver an additional unit of output to domestic final demand. Direct demand for IL. (Israeli pounds) 1,000 of 'Basic chemicals', for example, generates indirect demand for inputs from 34 of the 42 sectors into which the Israeli economy is broken down in the matrix – including an input of products worth IL. 266 from 'Basic chemicals' itself (see illustration below). Similarly, direct demand for IL. 1,000 of output from the 'Fish, meat, dairy products' sector calls for the input of IL. 725 of 'Livestock' and IL. 292 of 'Grains, fodder', along with numerous inputs of smaller value from other sectors. It should be noted that the direct demand for 'Basic chemicals' generates an indirect demand of IL. 5 on the 'Fish, meat, dairy products' sector and, reciprocally, that the direct demand for 'Fish, meat, dairy products' sets up an indirect demand for IL. 70 of 'Basic chemicals'. In these computations it is not necessary to distinguish between imports and domestic production, because the coefficients remain constant, whether the inputs are imported or produced at home. With the computations run for all sectors it is possible to determine the total outputs required of the entire economy in order to allow each domestic industry to satisfy the domestic final demand for its products.

The final demand to be met from within the Israeli economy is displayed as a series of tinted blocks running across the top of the chart on the pull-out. As in the input-output table on the pull-out, the country's exports are added (as grey extensions) to the tops of the blocks; the imports, represented by blocks of hatched lines, are subtracted. This presentation shows vividly how much the Israeli economy depends on imports, with blocks of hatched lines cutting deep into the tinted blocks and even descending below them in the six sectors where the imports required to satisfy in-direct demands exceed final demand.

The Israeli economy in the hypothetical state of self-sufficiency is represented by the row of coloured blocks of

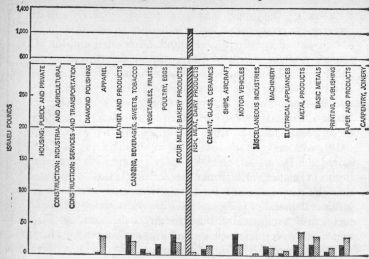

INDIRECT DEMAND generated in Israeli economy by 'direct' or final demand for IL. 1,000 worth of products from 'Basic chemicals' (*white bar*) and 'Fish, meat, diary products' (*diagonally striped bar*) sectors is shown here. Inputs from other industries to these sectors (*shown as crosshatched and black bars respectively*) needed to satisfy indirect demand were computed from input-coefficients for these sectors. Reference to the Israeli input-output table on the pull-out shows that many of these inputs ('Grains, fodder' particularly) are drawn from imports. Note that direct demand on

equal height that runs across the chart just below. Although they represent sectors of greatly different magnitude, all the blocks in this chart are of equal height because the vertical scale represents 'Per cent of self-sufficiency' and the monetary dimensions of the sectors are shown on the horizontal scale. The area of each block thus represents the total output required of that sector in order to satisfy the direct and indirect demands of the Israeli economy at self-sufficiency. The per cent allocated directly to final demand in each case is indicated by the height of the corresponding final-demand block in the row of blocks above.

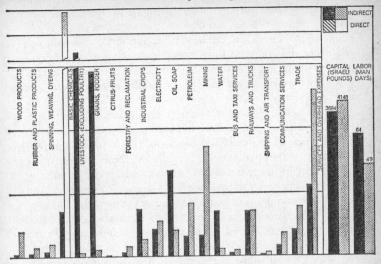

each sector generates indirect demand for its own products. Similar input-coefficient 'modules' constructed for all sectors of the economy make it possible to compute the total output required to satisfy the direct and indirect demand generated by any given level of final demand or by any given volume of exports or by import-replacing outputs from domestic industries, as shown in 'sky line' chart of the Israeli economy and other economies on the chart on the pull-out.

As a matter of fact, with the combination of labour, capital, and natural resources available to it in 1958, the year on which these hypothetical computations are based, the Israeli economy could not possibly have produced sufficient amounts of all the different kinds of goods and services that directly or indirectly were required to maintain the actual consumption and investment levels of the economy in that year. Domestic final demand was nonetheless maintained at those levels through recourse to foreign trade. By raising some outputs above the requirements of domestic direct and indirect demand, the country produced exportable surpluses.

In other sectors imports filled the gap between domestic output and the total direct and indirect demand of the economy. In Israel and elsewhere imports serve to economize resources that happen to be comparatively scarce, whereas exports provide a way to put to good use other resources that would otherwise be less effectively employed or perhaps not employed at all.

The crucial relation between foreign trade and the structure of the Israeli economy can best be assessed in two steps. To the tops of the coloured blocks of the hypothetical self-sufficient system are added grey blocks; these represent the direct and indirect demand that would have to be met by each sector in order to produce from domestic resources, and without drawing on imports, the exports shown by the grey blocks in the final-demand row above. As might be expected, some sectors are called on to increase their outputs, even though none or scarcely any of this output goes directly into exports. The substantial increase in the output of 'Grains, fodder', for example, would be accounted for in part at least by the indirect demand set up by exports of 'Fish, meat, dairy products', in accordance with the input-coefficient shown in the chart on pages 142 and 143.

The next step takes account of the effect of imports. The effect is analogous to that of exports, but it works in the opposite direction. An import of IL. 1,000 worth of 'Basic chemicals' for example, not only eliminates directly the demand for an equal amount of 'Basic chemicals' from the domestic industry but also, as shown in the chart on pages 142 and 143, reduces the indirect demand for the products of thirty-three other industries and 'Basic chemicals' as well. From the input-coefficients for all sectors, hatched blocks are now constructed to represent the amount of each kind of goods that would be required, directly and indirectly, to produce in Israel the bill of imports shown in the final-demand row at the top of the chart. These theoretical import-replacing outputs are subtracted from the total height of the coloured and grey blocks in the self-sufficiency row. The lowered and irregular 'sky line' thereby established shows the actual output of the Israeli economy from sector to sector as a per cent of the level of output that would give the country self-sufficiency.

The fact that so few sectors of the Israeli economy rise above the self-sufficiency horizon and that so many fall below it is explained to a great extent by the relatively large amount of foreign aid received by the country. In addition to offsetting the export-import deficit, such aid also permits the country to substitute capital indirectly for labour. As the bar graph at the right-hand end of the chart of the hypothetical self-sufficient Israeli economy shows, the attainment of actual self-sufficiency would require a larger outlay of labour than of capital.

These considerations undoubtedly also apply to resources, although lack of sufficiently detailed information at present makes it impossible to establish the precise relation between domestic resources and the structure of the Israeli (or any other) economy. In connexion with resources it should be remarked that no economy can be completely self-sufficient. As employed in the present analysis, self-sufficiency should be taken to mean the state of development at which non-replaceable imports are covered by the exports needed to pay for them. The sky line in the chart indicates that the Israeli economy still falls well below self-sufficiency thus defined. Foreign aid makes it possible, however, for Israel to maintain not only a much higher level of domestic consumption than it could have achieved otherwise but also a much higher rate of investment and growth towards mature development.

The same chart presents analogous sky lines for the U.S. economy and for the underdeveloped economies of Egypt and Peru. Comparison of one of these countries to another must be qualified because of the differences in the way their statisticians have aggregated the various industries of each country into sectors. The sectors are arrayed, however, in each profile in the same sequence in which they should and let us hope – will eventually appear on a triangulated input-output table of the economic system of the entire world.

In common with Israel, it can be seen, Egypt and Peru present jagged total-output profiles, with many sectors falling short of the self-sufficiency line. The U.S. profile, in contrast, is flat and averages out somewhat above self-sufficiency. This is a reflection of the country's mature development: its favourable balance of trade and the additional outflow of foreign aid-in-kind. The chart also demonstrates, incidentally, that the celebrated unfavourable balance of payments and the worrisome weakness of the dollar are the result of paper transactions.

Each of the underdeveloped countries specializes in the massive export of a few agricultural and mineral commodities and depends on imports for the supply of a broad spectrum of manufactured goods. (The diamond-polishing industry of Israel is worthy of special mention: established in that country by refugees from Nazism, it serves a comparatively minuscule domestic final demand and earns significant foreign credits to cover imports.) The U.S. economy, on the other hand, exports a great diversity of manufactured goods and imports a few agricultural and mineral commodities. An underdeveloped economy is consequently the mirror-image of an advanced economy.

Comparison of the four national economic structures reveals a striking hierarchy based on the ratio of agriculture to total economic activity. The agricultural and food sectors of the United States, although they far outproduce those of the other countries, constitute only about 15 per cent of the country's total output. Israel comes next, with about 24 per cent of its total activity in agriculture, then Egypt with 36 per cent, and Peru with 40 per cent. This may serve as a fair index of their different degrees of development.

The sky lines of the three underdeveloped countries, instead of displaying random ups and downs, are characterized by gradual transitions from clearly defined high plateaux to well-formed valleys. This is no accident: the sectors that approach one another in height represent groups of industries closely related by their inter-industry transactions. In the Israeli profile, for example, there are obvious connexions in the three-step order of the 'Metal products', 'Electrical appliances', and 'Machinery' sectors, which are stated more explicitly at the intersections of their rows and columns in the input-output table.

Economic systems tend naturally to combine the international division of labour with the minimization of transportation costs. The latter costs can be kept down if an industry is located or developed in close proximity to the largest direct customers for its outputs or to the suppliers of its inputs. Quite independently of transportation costs, however, a growing economy derives a considerable, although less measurable, advantage from developing whole families of structurally related industries rather than isolated industries that depend on foreign trade for supplies and markets. The incessant process of technological change derives strong stimulus from close association between sellers and buyers, between the maker and the potential user of a new process or product. As an economy passes from one phase of its development to another, 'block reaction' will cause low blocks to grow tall, whereas blocks that now protrude above the sky line will gradually lose their domineering stature.

Developmental evolution along these lines is illustrated by the comparison of the actual profile of the Peruvian economy for 1955 with the hypothetical profile of that economy for 1965; this projection is based on the projections of the United Nations Economic Commission for Latin America (see chart on pull-out). The upward shift of the self-sufficiency horizon reflects a large increase in the over-all level of final domestic demand. This upward shift is accompanied by a horizontal displacement of the sectors from left to right that reflects the faster growth of the industrial sectors in relation to that of the agricultural sectors. Dependence on imports is diminished, although the same commodities continue to account for the bulk of the country's imports. Agriculture, basic metals, and the extractive industries continue to provide, directly and indirectly, the exportable surpluses. As the result of rapid industrial growth, however, the profile shows that Peru will cease to be an exporter of petroleum and coal and will become, for a while at least, an importer of these fuels.

Input-output analysis thus makes it possible to project changes in the structure of a developing economy in terms of the underlying composition of domestic consumption and investment, exports, and imports. The predetermined coefficients of inputs required directly and indirectly to deliver each type of goods and service to final demand provide modules that can be combined in many different ways to draft internally consistent blueprints for the future. The mere existence of an elaborate projection will not, of course, bring about economic growth. Much political acumen and drive, much sweat and tears go into the actual realization even of the best-conceived development plan. Progress, however, will be faster along a road well mapped in advance, and the cost of progress in terms of labour, capital, and human sacrifice considerably less.

The Development of Nigeria

WOLFGANG F. STOLPER

How Nigeria, the most populous nation of Africa, has launched its advance towards self-sustaining growth.

On 29 March, 1962, the Federal Finance Minister of Nigeria, Chief the Honourable Festus Sam Okotie-Eboh, rose in the Nigerian Parliament to make his annual budget speech. 'I can see a vision', he said, 'of a new and prosperous Nigeria – a Nigeria whose blood is virile and whose aspirations are fired by noble objectives. The sleeping giant of Africa is awake and determined to take her rightful place marching with the rest of humanity.'

Okotie-Eboh has a habit of naming his annual budgets, and he chose 'Mobilization' for this one – which covered the fiscal year to 31 March 1963 – because Nigeria was about to embark on its first National Development Plan, to take effect on 1 April, 1962, and to continue for six years. 'For the very first time in our history', Okotie-Eboh said, 'an effort [is] being made to look at the resources and the priorities from an ... all-Nigeria perspective.'

The plan embodies a bold and fateful undertaking. Nigeria is an underdeveloped country in an early stage of the development process: newly independent of a political colonialism but continuing in what amounts to an economic colonialism because of its dependence on a few material exports and many manufactured imports; long on agriculture and manpower but short on manufacturing and skills; rich in potential but still far from its proclaimed goal of 'a modern, diversified and virtually self-sustaining [economic] system'.

Much depends on the success of this and subsequent plans. Nigeria is a democracy patterned on British lines. It is also the largest Negro nation. If it can build roads and industries, bring electricity to its villages, and educate its youth while safeguarding its internal liberties and external borders, it will set an example that other African nations may well follow. Moreover, success would kill once and for all the pervasive thesis that the Negro is innately incapable of organizing a modern society. If Nigeria fails, the equally pernicious belief that only authoritarianism can provide an effective road to development may gain a universal hold in Africa, and the champions of apartheid will be emboldened.

Nigeria is a big country. Its population of between 35 and 40 million is the largest in Africa. It also ranks among the larger African nations in territory: 356,500 square miles, which is slightly more than the area of Texas and Oklahoma combined. Beyond the bare statistics, Nigeria is a country of great variety – in its geography, people, politics, and economics.

Geographically Nigeria has four distinct regions. Along the coast, which is close to the Equator, is a region of torrid, swampy lowlands. Here the delta draining Africa's largest river system, the main streams of which are the Niger and the Benue, is cut by scores of channels into hundreds of islands. Farther inland is a belt of dense rain forest, largely composed of cottonwoods, mahogany, satinwoods, and cedars. To the north of the forests lies the vast grassy plain that forms most of Nigeria. The forest and the southern part of the savanna country are suitable for growing cocoa, rubber, rice, yams, cassava, and oil palms but are inhospitable to cattle because of the tsetse fly. In the northern savanna there is herding of cattle, sheep and goats and successful cultivation of cotton, soybeans, millet, Guinea corn, and peanuts (which the Nigerians, like the British, call groundnuts). The fourth geographical region, in the far north, is thorn forest and near-desert.

Throughout much of the country appear significant mineral deposits. Petroleum, recently discovered in the delta, has rapidly become one of the country's major exports. On the central plateau are tin and columbite, a black mineral that yields the increasingly useful metal columbium. Coal, with indicated reserves of 240 million tons, is found in several places, but it is of low grade: there are also considerable deposits of limestone and iron ore.

The people of Nigeria belong to a homogeneous racial group. There are, however, some 250 different tribes, ranging from millions of individuals to a few thousand, and almost every tribe has its own language. Since 'tribe' is anthropologically a rather vague term, the British administration in Nigeria sought to clarify the situation there by defining a Nigerian tribe as 'one or more clans descended from one legendary ancestor, though the legend may have been lost; originally observing one common shrine, though the memory may have been lost; speaking one language, though perhaps not the same dialect, and enlarged by assimilated peoples'. In the absence of a common Nigerian tongue English serves as the official language and as somewhat of a lingua franca, known at least by the educated. Another result of the tribal profusion is diversity of religions. Christianity predominates in the south, the result of more than a century of missionary activity, and Islam in the north, the result of incursions from North Africa centuries ago. Throughout the country pagan religions survive in large number and variety.

Politically, Nigeria is divided into three autonomous regions: Northern, Eastern, and Western. A fourth region, the Midwest, is in process of establishment; it will consist of the provinces of Benin and Delta, which are now part of the Western Region. There is also a small federal territory centering on Lagos, the national capital. Each of the three existing regions has a predominant tribal group, several other distinguishing characteristics, and a strong regional pride.

The Northern Region, the capital of which is Kaduna, is the largest, both in area (281,782 square miles) and in population (some 20 million). Its predominant tribal grouping is the Hausa-Fulani, an alliance, strengthened by intermarriage, in which the Hausas are the more numerous but the Fulani are the ruling element. The North is a world apart from the other regions; it is the Moslem area, with conservative politics and a feudal social system in which power lies with the Moslem emirs chosen from noble families. But it is also an area with great political realism, a sense of the urgency of change, and a determination to bring it about. The dominant political party is the Northern People's Congress, headed by Alhaji Sir Ahmadu Bello, considered by many the most powerful man in the nation.

In the Eastern Region, of which the capital is Enugu, the Ibo is the dominant tribe and the National Convention of Nigerian Citizens the dominant party. A leading figure in the party is Nnamdi Azikiwe, the Governor-General of Nigeria and the grand old man of Nigerian nationalism. With 8 to 10 million people in its territory of 29,484 square miles, the Eastern Region is the most densely populated area in the country. Its population has a reputation for energy and resourcefulness.

The Western Region is populated mainly by the Yoruba, who are traditionally town dwellers; this is reflected in the fact that the urban population of the region (people living in cities of more than 20,000) is about 30 per cent, in contrast to 7 per cent in the East and 4 per cent in the North. Ibadan, the capital of the Western Region, is the largest Negro city in Africa, with probably a million inhabitants; it is also the seat of University College Ibadan, the Federal University of Nigeria. The Western Region has an area of 45,376 square miles and a population estimated in 1961 at 7.1 million. In politics, unlike the other regions, there has always been a strong opposition in the regional parliament. The Action Group, headed by Chief Obafemi Awolowo, was once dominant but split a year ago, and during a brief interregnum a federal administrator ran the region; the regional government now consists of a coalition between an Action Group bloc (the United Peoples

Party) and the National Convention of Nigerian Citizens.

The major exclusive responsibilities of the regional governments are agriculture and education below the college level. These governments obtain most of the revenue they raise themselves (as distinct from what the federal government gives them) from agricultural products – either as export duties, produce sales taxes, or profits of the Marketing Boards, which buy the major export crops from producers at prices substantially below those obtaining in the world market.

At the federal level the Northern People's Congress has an absolute majority in Parliament and is the senior member of the coalition government headed by Alhaji Sir Abubakar Tafawa Balewa (a member of the party) as prime minister. The other partner in the coalition is the National Convention of Nigerian Citizens. Formerly the Action Group constituted the loyal opposition; since the split in that party and the arrest of Awolowo, its leader in Parliament, on charges of treason, the opposition has had no clear spokesman.

Underlying the political relations at the federal level is considerable tension, originating principally in regional and tribal jealousies. Efforts by the major parties to expand outside their own regions have met rebuffs, and the parties have therefore tended to become increasingly regional in outlook.

These political differences, reinforced by regional pride and autonomy, exert a centrifugal influence on the federation. Nevertheless, there is a strong Nigerian national consciousness, and there are powerful unifying forces. One is the heritage of British law, parliamentary government, and civil service, together with the unifying effect of the English language. Moreover, the federal government has exclusive responsibility for national defence, foreign affairs, and the money system; it operates the railroads, the major ports, and many other enterprises through statutory corporations that have actual or virtual monopolies and function throughout the Federation; it is responsible for the main highways and the communication system, and it provides approximately two thirds of the revenue received by the regional governments.

Economically, Nigeria, like all parliamentary democracies, is a mixture of public and private enterprise. The latter is extensive but tends to gravitate towards small-scale activities; large ventures are more often undertaken by the government or by expatriate business.

Nigeria's economy received a substantial impetus in the one hundred years of British rule, although more as a result of normal colonial enterprise and trade than through any deliberate policy to achieve 'economic development'. By 1911 the country had a railway from Lagos to Kano. The road system by 1960, the year of independence, had grown to 46,761 miles, of which 5,267 were paved. The state-owned Electricity Corporation generated 448.3 million kilowatt-hours of power in 1960, a better than thirtyfold increase over 1937.

It was also significant for Nigeria's development that the British for many years pursued a policy of making colonies pay for themselves. In contrast to the attitude adopted by the French towards their African colonies, the British made no systematic attempt to provide a sheltered market for Nigerian exports – a policy that, whatever its shortcomings, had the advantage of keeping Nigerian exports competitive. Under this policy Nigeria emerged from World War II with substantial sterling assets (mostly accumulated by the Marketing Boards), and it also was in a position to finance its own ordinary budget and make substantial capital investments out of budget surpluses.

Towards the end of the British period there were some attemps at systematic, planned development at the government level to supplement the build-up of Nigeria under private enterprise. In 1929 and 1940 the British Parliament passed Colonial Development and Welfare acts, but they did not really get off the ground, because of the depression and the war. In 1945 a third act made £120 million available to all the colonies in the period from 1946 to 1957; each colony was asked to produce a ten-year development plan. In terms of the need these efforts did not go very far, but they constituted at least a beginning.

How much this move towards systematic development quickened the growth of Nigeria is difficult to say, because of the lack of adequate statistics on the economy before 1950. It is a matter of record, however, that there was substantial growth during the 1950s. In terms of 1957 prices the gross domestic product of 1950 was about £699.3 million (the Nigerian pound, like the British, is equivalent to $2.80) and in 1960 about £1,023 million – an average increase of approximately 4 per cent a year, which is good by the standards of underdeveloped countries. Gross fixed investment (in roads, schools, housing, plant, and other fixed capital assets) rose from about 7 per cent of gross domestic product in 1950 to more than 15 per cent in 1960 – also a considerable achievement. During the decade consumer expenditures rose from £609.4 million to £870 million; that rise exceeded any possible population increase and therefore represented an improvement in the average standard of living.

The increase in the real goods provided during this period showed the more concrete aspects of the abstraction represented by the term 'gross domestic product'. The output of cement, textiles, and many other consumer products increased many times. The number of telephones in service increased from 7,760 to 38,690. Port cargo doubled (to 7.31 million tons) and railroad freight rose 50 per cent (to 1,250 million ton-miles). Spending on education increased from £3.1 million in 1950 to £26.3 million in 1960.

In 1959, a year before independence, the Nigerian government issued what amounted to a formal portrait of the economy: *Economic Survey of Nigeria*. It indicated that a majority of the population lived in rural areas and that 75 per cent of the adult labour force worked in agriculture, forestry, and animal husbandry; that the cultivation of field and tree crops accounted for 50 per cent of the national income and 85 per cent of the country's exports, in addition to enabling Nigeria to feed itself. The survey observed that 'the prospects for raising the wealth of the country and the level of the National Income rest largely on the possibilities of increasing exports and developing industry'. With respect to exports the survey foresaw 'good grounds for hoping that oil exports will become important', as they have, but cautioned that 'it is to agricultural production that Nigeria must look for some time to come for any major increase in export earnings'. On the subject of industry, which was described as 'not yet a major contributor to Nigeria's national income', the survey said:

It is a major objective of Government policy to promote the growth of industry in Nigeria, both to increase the wealth of the country and to provide new sources of employment. Industrialization will also help to make Nigeria less dependent on the relation between the world prices for the primary products which she exports and manufactured goods, nearly all of which she at present imports.

Some of the other statistics showed how far Nigeria had to travel on the development road. Her per capita income of less than £30 a year put her in the lowest 20 per cent of the one hundred areas in the world classified as under-developed, and even that income was unevenly distributed among the regions. Illiteracy was high; the 1952–3 census had reported only 12 per cent of the population as being literate, and although that figure rose somewhat thereafter, the educational attainments of the population still fell considerably short of the requirements for industrial development. By now, in the two southern regions, about 80 per cent of the school-age children are in elementary schools. But Nigeria was and is particularly short in high-level manpower: entrepreneurs, administrators, and all manner of professional and technical people. In fact, skills are the country's greatest need.

Also reflecting the country's underdeveloped status was the composition of the labour force and imports. Not only was the greater part of the labour force engaged in agriculture but also nearly 60 per cent of those so engaged were producing primarily for subsistence rather than the market. Imports, according to a study by Ojetunde Aboyade of University College Ibadan, consisted in 1959 of 48 per cent soft consumers' goods, 10 per cent durable consumers' goods, 30 per cent capital goods, 11 per cent processing and raw materials, and 1 per cent miscellaneous imports.

At a more abstract level past developments showed some other disquieting facts. As the rate of investment in development had increased, a substantial export surplus had changed in 1954 to an import surplus. Sterling assets had thereafter dropped from £263.1 million in March 1955, to £147.5 million in December 1961. The balance of payments would therefore have to be watched.

The rate of domestic savings had meanwhile remained at about 10 per cent of gross domestic product. That was a high rate for an underdeveloped country. But with sterling reserves falling, capital investment could be maintained at a high level only through increased domestic savings or increased capital imports. The former, however, would require a considerable effort and could, through an increased tax burden, produce heavy political repercussions, whereas the latter would affect the balance of payments adversely by increasing the amount of money needed to service the external debt.

Finally, the increase in the gross domestic product had begun to slow down. Some of this was the result of falling prices for the country's raw-material exports and some the effect of adverse weather on agricultural output. But part of the responsibility clearly lay in the fact that some of the past capital expenditures had been for projects that were slow to produce results.

These facts set the context for thinking about the National Development Plan in the interregional Joint Planning

Committee and its secretariat, the Federal Ministry of Economic Development, where I headed the Economic Planning Unit for eighteen months under a grant from the Ford Foundation. The declining growth rate, the prospect of still lower export prices, the drop in sterling balances, and the need to increase the mobilization of domestic resources for development all pointed to one conclusion: it was essential to put more emphasis than past development efforts had on directly productive investments and less on 'social overhead', which includes education, health, and housing.

From this determination it also followed that we would have to emphasize the central role of the ordinary annual budget, which the Nigerians call the recurrent budget. This meant viewing the development problem as involving the mobilization and allocation of resources. It also meant resisting any attempt to see development as essentially a problem of governmental and private capital formation, or to separate development expenditures from non-development expenses prematurely. Every capital project builds up additional recurrent expenditures; even if a hospital is a gift, the recurrent budget must provide the money for the staff. In addition, some of the most powerful development expenditures – such as for agricultural and industrial services, which will raise productivity and product faster than any other categories of governmental outlay – are always included in the recurrent budget.

There was, therefore, a close relation between the recurrent budget and the size of the government's capital programme. The recurrent budget also provided a major link with the private sector, since policies on such matters as subsidies and taxes have a direct impact on the budget.

Another of our basic principles was to view our role as one of coordinating and helping rather than imposing a central will. To a certain extent this was inescapable because of Nigeria's federalized structure and the strong sense of autonomy in the regions. But we also wanted to evoke the interest and draw on the experience of the people at

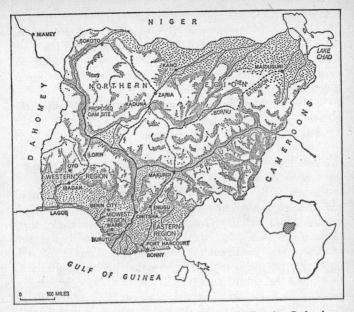

MAJOR POLITICAL and physical features of Nigeria. Only three of the regions, which have a role comparable to that of the American states, now exist; the Midwest Region is in process of formation following a plebiscite in July (1963).

the grass roots in order to bring as many as possible into the development process. We thought it absurd in any case for a man sitting in Lagos or any of the regional capitals to pretend to know in sufficient detail such matters as the agricultural problems in the Lake Chad area. We therefore emphasized development of the planning framework from below and the decentralization of decision-making in the execution of the plan.

The National Development Plan as finally evolved includes coordinated undertakings by the federal government and each of the three regions. Total government capital expenditures envisioned over the six years of the first plan are £676.8 million, of which 71.4 per cent is to be apportioned to 'economic development', meaning the directly productive sectors of the economy such as agriculture, trade, industry, electricity, and communications; 20.8 per cent to social overhead; and 7.8 per cent to administration, a category that includes defence.

In the economic-development sector of the plan the greatest outlay – £143.8 million, or 21.3 per cent of the total plan expenditure – will go to the transport system. The greater part of that outlay will be federal, directed chiefly towards highway improvement, port development, and expansion of the national railroad system.

Electricity will receive £101.7 million, or 15.1 per cent of the plan total. Virtually all the outlay will be federal, and two thirds of that will go towards what is in effect the cornerstone of the plan – the Niger dams project. The broad aim of that project is the establishment of a nationwide electricity grid and the comprehensive development of the river that gives the country its name; the first stage, which the current plan includes, is the construction of a dam at Kainji. The second stage calls for a dam at Jebba by 1982. and the third stage for a dam at Shiroro Gorge. The total installed capacity, once the three stages have been completed, will be 1.73 million kilowatts.

The Kainji Dam is the largest single project in the first plan. In many ways it epitomizes Nigeria's efforts towards integrated development of her natural resources. It will provide electricity for all parts of the country. It will improve navigation on the main rivers, thereby lowering transport costs and providing easier access to the interior from the sea. It will regulate floods and help agriculture, but it will pay on electricity alone.

The category of 'primary production', which includes agriculture, livestock, forestry, and fishing, will receive £91.7 million, or 13.6 per cent of the plan total. A third of that will be spent by the Eastern Region, the remainder in approximately equal shares by the other two regions and the federal government. The money will go for such undertakings as research, training, irrigation, crop improvement, farm settlements and plantations, and a fishing harbour at Lagos. On this subject the plan observes:

> The expansion and modernisation of agriculture and related production is of crucial importance to the development of the Nigerian economy. The proceeds from export products will determine to a large extent the volume of imports which can be made available for economic development in other sectors; the efficient expansion of domestic food production will determine not only whether the Nigerian people will eat better but also whether they can effectively reduce dependence on imported foodstuffs; the increased productivity of agriculture will determine whether the income of the great majority of the people can be effectively raised and this will in turn determine the size of the domestic market for the new industries which are expected to spring up.

The final major category of economic-development expenditure is 'trade and industry', which will receive £90.2 million, or 13.4 per cent of the total. About half of that spending will be federal; regional outlays will range from £23.4 million in the Western Region to £9.9 million in the Northern Region. Chief among the projects is the construction of an iron and steel mill at a site as yet to be determined; it is expected to cost £30 million and to be in operation by 1966 at the earliest. The mill is envisioned as being the centre of a complex that will provide an extensive stimulus to the economy by using Nigerian ores, limestone, electricity, oil, and coal, in addition to producing upward of 125,000 tons of steel products annually for the growing economy and thereby reducing the country's dependence on imported steel.

Another major project in the trade-and-industry category is an oil refinery under construction at Port Harcourt by a combine of the Shell oil group and the British Petroleum Company Limited, which are sharing the £8 million cost with the four governments. Ultimate ownership of the refinery will be 40 per cent in the hands of the Nigerian government, 40 per cent Shell and British Petroleum, and 20 per cent Nigerian stockholders. The refinery will be profitable and will also result in substantial import savings, with outlays for petroleum imports expected to drop from £11.7 million this year to £3.4 million by 1965, when the refinery will be fully in operation.

This portion of the plan also provides for the establishment of a National Development Bank 'to join foreign skills and experience and foreign private capital with Nigerian skills and capital in the development of new industries and the expansion of existing ones'. This bank is coming into existence during 1963. In addition there is provision for an array of technical and advisory services for Nigerian private industry. Outlays of £30 million for communications, mainly the telephone system, and £24.3 million for drinking and industrial water projects complete the economic-development section of the plan.

In the social-overhead sector of the plan the largest outlay will be for education, which will receive £69.8 million, or 10.3 per cent of the plan total. The programme calls for substantial expansion of teacher training and school capacity at all levels. Town and country planning will receive £41.7 million and health measures £17 million.

The financing of the plan depends heavily on foreign aid, which is expected to supply fully half the need. The Nigerian federal and regional governments hope to have £263 million available from their own resources towards the £653.8 million in planned capital expenditure (that figure being the £676.8 million in capital projects outlined by the plan less £23 million in 'underspending', that is, a predictable shortfall). There is therefore a gap of £389.8 million, of which £327.1 million is to be covered by 'assumed foreign aid' and the remainder is so far 'uncovered'. The Nigerians hope that they can eliminate the uncovered gap by budgetary economies.

Nigeria's development also will continue to depend heavily on private investment, which hitherto has been slightly greater than public investment. The plan contemplates that two thirds of the total gross investment will come from government funds and one third from private sources. This does not reflect any political bias, however; in fact, it is expected that private investment will provide more and public investment less than outlined in the plan. The private investment anticipated by the plan over the six years is at least £400 million, about half of it from abroad. Achievement of that objective will require an increase of at least 10 per cent over present levels of foreign private investment in Nigeria and constitutes one of the major challenges of the plan.

This first plan is an ambitious one – I think overly ambitious. Something of this appears in the results of the first year, although they also reflect the inevitable delays and difficulties involved in setting so big a venture in motion.

By the end of that year commitments of foreign aid came to only £105.5 million – £80 million committed by the United States before the plan went into effect, £15 million from Great Britain, £8.5 million from West Germany, and £2 million from Switzerland. A substantial loan from the International Bank for Reconstruction and Development towards the Kainji Dam is expected. Nevertheless, substantially more will be needed. In the development of capital projects during the first year, governmental and private investments were approximately equal. Investment in the economic-development sector was £46 million, or about £9 million below the plan target; within that sector investment in the highly productive area of agriculture fell short but investment in transport (notably roads and bridges) was considerably in excess of plan targets. Total expenditure in the social-overhead sector at £18 million was some £2.5 million above the plan target, even though relatively little was spent in the high-priority field of education and relatively much on health projects. Administrative expenses were almost double the projected amount because of the unforeseen amount of expenditure on national defence, which has joined agriculture, industry, and technical education as a major plan priority.

Moreover, recurrent expenditures rose sharply, moving Okotie-Eboh to remark in his 1963 budget speech that he was 'deeply concerned'. Exports fell by about £3 million because timber and palm-product shipments dropped in both volume and price, the cocoa price fell drastically, and the cotton crop was halved by adverse weather. The effort to tap domestic savings had results that Okotie-Eboh called 'disappointing'.

There were, however, some bright spots. Imports in 1962 dropped by £20 million, or about 10 per cent, and the greater part of the decline was in such consumers' goods as textiles, clothing, household utensils, and beer. In contrast, imports of capital goods and machinery rose significantly. As a result the balance-of-payments position improved and imports shifted towards those contributing directly to development. In addition to this encouraging trend private investment had done well and many public projects got off to a good start.

Nigerian development is indeed gathering way, but there are some shoal waters in its course. A major deficiency in the output of university graduates and persons of intermediate education to reduce the dearth of skilled manpower appears inevitable. Frederick Harbison (see 'Education for Development', page 118) has estimated that Nigeria needs 2,000 university graduates a year, whereas only 1,000 Nigerians are receiving university degrees at home or abroad and that the annual requirement for persons with a secondary school education is 4,000 more than the 1,500 the school system is producing. At the same time, ironically, the country has a growing problem of 'school-leavers' – primary school graduates who are not equipped for any government or business jobs but who flock to the towns looking for them fruitlessly.

There is also the possibility of dangerous distortion in development priorities. Although directly productive projects are often difficult, showpiece projects that have no direct effect on economic growth are often easy. The results of the first year indicate a tendency to drift towards them.

Political stresses also may affect the development process. Nigeria has become a republic along Indian lines, and the transition has produced strains. It also remains a possibility that the regional balance, already somewhat disturbed by Northern domination and the creation of the Midwest state, may change further towards complete Northern rule for the country.

In contrast, however, was the outcome of a recent discussion about adopting a preventive-detention act — the device so many authoritarian governments have used to suppress political opposition. Nigeria's rejection of that idea is strong evidence of the deep root that liberty has taken and of the moderation and strong sense of direction of the national leadership

Nigeria has great potential and a strong determination to develop it. Her goal of becoming self-sustaining is attainable, and she should eventually reach it. How long that will take is difficult to say. My estimate, which many Nigerians consider unduly pessimistic, is that it will require at least a generation.

The Development of India

PITAMBAR PANT

With a diversified population of 450 million, India has perhaps the most complex problem of development. It seeks to advance by methods that follow its traditional avoidance of coercion.

India joined the community of twentieth-century nation-states in 1947, the second largest in population and the seventh in land area. The people had won their independence in a struggle unique for its stress on peaceful means. From the beginning of the struggle the national leadership, under Mahatma Gandhi, recognized that the pledges of the independence movement would not be redeemed until the mass of the people were assured work, a tolerable standard of life, and opportunity for continued advancement. Today the country is committed to a crucial experiment in economic development. India believes that industrialization and the attendant radical reconstruction of society can be achieved fairly rapidly and without reliance on class hatred or the invocation of violence and coercion.

This belief is a matter of faith; history offers no clear precedent to support it. In the past, revolutionary violence offered the only path to radical social change, and in those days the pace of the underlying change in the living conditions of people was generally slow. In our time, however, the advance of science and technology, the better knowledge of social and economic processes, and an improved climate of international cooperation have brought material prosperity within the reach of all people. And political democracy has brought with it the possibility of peaceful change.

India is now in the second year of the third in a succession of five-year plans that are guiding its development. Its 450 million citizens – nearly a sixth of the population of the world, speaking a multiplicity of languages, cherishing a diversity of cultural traditions, and still segregated in a multitude of castes – live in fifteen states and eight territories that constitute the Indian Union. Yet change is already and everywhere apparent. The jet airplane flying overhead is as much a part of the landscape as the bullock cart carrying produce from village to town. The thatched mud huts of villages in the Punjab surround the modern capital at Chandigarh designed by the French architect Le Corbusier. While the atom is being harnessed at Tarapur to supply energy from a reactor of advanced design, cow dung will continue to be burned as the primary source of fuel in millions of Indian homes. India has many scientific laboratories and outstanding scientists, but the astrologer remains a respected member of society.

Of India's total area of 809 million acres, one fifth is under forest and two fifths are under cultivation. About 20 per cent of the cultivated area is irrigated. Of the cropped area 80 per cent is used for producing cereal grains and pulses (the seeds of leguminous plants such as peas and beans). These constitute the staple food, and because the farming is largely for sheer subsistence they are grown everywhere. The kind grown – whether rice, wheat, barley, and maize or the indigenous *jowar, ragi,* or *bajra* – depends on the local climate, soil, and availability of water. Cash crops include tea, coffee, sugar cane, oilseeds, tobacco, jute and cotton, spices, and tropical fruits. Jute and cotton manufactures, tea, tobacco, and spices account for nearly half the export earnings of India.

Lack of water at the right time is the principal handicap and hazard to Indian agriculture. The rains are seasonal monsoons coming once or twice a year; they are undependable from year to year. Most of the rain comes in the summer and floods to the sea in rivers further swollen by the melting of the Himalayan snows. A scanty monsoon can seriously damage the chief harvest of the year.

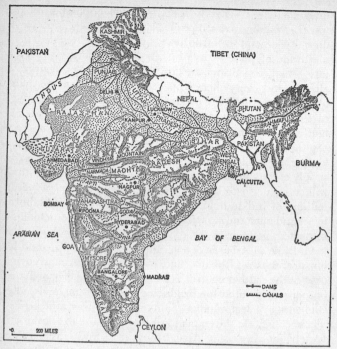

MODERN INDIA, a country of 1,264,900 square miles, has a population of 450 million – nearly a sixth of the population of the world.

In recent years Indian planning has laid great stress on irrigation. With irrigation not only is the main harvest assured but also two or three crops a year are possible. At present an estimated 70 million acres are under irrigation; some of the land has been irrigated for ages past. About 40 million acres get water from wells, tanks, and minor works, and 30 million acres are supplied by large and medium-sized projects. Another 100 million acres are believed to be irrigable by the development of ground-water supplies and the abundant but unharnessed river waters.

India has most of the mineral resources necessary for its industrial development. It has one of the largest reserves of high-quality iron ore in the world, estimated at 21,000 million tons. The supply of coking coal, estimated at 2,000 million tons, is not large but is sufficient for the development of substantial steel production by established technology. Bauxite, the chief ore of aluminium, is fairly widely distributed in high-grade deposits. India is one of the largest producers of manganese and has a virtual monopoly of mica mining. There are also fair reserves of limestone, gypsum, refractory materials, ilmenite (titanium ore), and some gold, copper, and minor minerals.

For energy resources the Indian economy can count on 50,000 million tons of coal down to the fully workable depth of 2,000 feet. Intensive oil exploration, initiated six years ago with the help chiefly of the U.S.S.R., has resulted in the discovery of new fields in Gujarat and Assam; domestic production of crude oil is expected to reach 7 million tons within a few years. The abundant monazite sands in Kerala provide a rich source of thorium for the development of atomic energy. Of the electric potential of the river waters, estimated at more than 40 million kilowatts, not even 10 per cent has yet been exploited.

Some 360 million Indians live in 570,000 small villages dotted all over the country. Although there are 2,690 towns and cities, only 107 have a population of more than 100,000; seven cities are large, having a population of more than one million each. The population of the towns is growing perhaps twice as fast as that of the country as a whole, with migration from villages playing an important part. Nearly 25,000 of the towns and villages had been electrified by 1961, compared with only 4,000 a decade earlier.

Agriculture engages 70 per cent of all male and female workers: 130 million out of a total of 188 million. It contributes nearly half the national income, but the average income per worker engaged in agriculture is only 40 per cent of the average income per worker in other sectors.

Manufacturing in organized factories contributes only 10 per cent to national income and employs fewer than 4 million workers.

As a consequence of India's population growth – nearly 2.5 per cent a year – half the population is less than twenty years old; persons over sixty years are less than 5 per cent of the total. By 1975 the working population is likely to number 250 million, four times the present labour force of the United States.

Today India is a poor nation. Poverty is not confined to groups of unfortunates or to backward regions; it engulfs almost the entire population. The average per capita product is barely $70 a year. The consumption of the poorest 10 per cent is as low as five cents a day and, notwithstanding the conspicuous consumption and the riches of a tiny minority at the top, the consumption of the richest 5 per cent aggregates no more than fifty cents a day. Mass poverty is associated with low output and low income per worker and with widespread under-employment of human and material resources.

In agriculture the yields per acre are low: in rice, one third that of Japan; in cotton, one fifth that of Egypt. The reason for the low yields is basically the use of poor agricultural technology. In the agricultural population there are wide disparities in income arising primarily out of the uneven distribution of land. Although the typical ceiling on ownership of land is about thirty acres, the number of persons who have tiny holdings of two acres or less runs into millions. With the best of effort and assuming substantial gains in future productivity per acre, the income of most farm families – and of the families of the landless agricultural workers – is not likely to approach an acceptable minimum within a reasonable period of time.

The majority of the non-agricultural population is not much better off. Occupations in the services and trades are overcrowded and do not provide adequate incomes. Large numbers are engaged in traditional village industries, handicrafts, or small manufacturing, using only simple tools and little or no power.

The large size of India's population makes the task of securing a rise in living standards much more difficult. To increase consumption of food grains by two ounces per head per day, for example, will require an increase of 9 million tons in annual supplies. This means an increase of more than 10 per cent in domestic production or alternatively an increase in import expenditures of $750 million, which is more than half of India's total export earnings. Similarly, to provide the 4 or 5 million new workers who join the labour force every year with capital equipment at the rate of $200 each adds up to $1,000 million a year – about equal to the foreign aid India expects to receive during its third five-year plan. Because of the high rate of population growth a good part of the investment is required merely to keep the average per capita income constant; only a part is available to increase per capita income.

The solution of these problems lies in transforming the technology of production in various fields and modernizing the economic institutions. The technical side of the task is to get technology from abroad firmly rooted in the Indian soil through the rapid extension of scientific education and research and the rapid build-up of productive facilities. The economic side of the problem is to mobilize the physical resources by fiscal and financial means. In order to support increased investment, increased savings are required. In other words, a larger proportion of current production has to be set aside for building a productive capacity designed to yield a larger flow of goods and services in the future.

It is a difficult and delicate problem in a democracy of poor people to raise the rate of savings fast enough. Income per head is low, and for the very large number the margin for reduction of current consumption is small. The savings of the few rich are not enough. In the parliamentary democracy of India, based on adult franchise, the government has undertaken to increase the rate of capital formation by persuasion and without accentuation of inequalities of income. Accepting these social and political limitations, India's planners envision an increase in the rate of domestic savings from 5 per cent of national income to 20 per cent over the twenty-five years from 1950 to 1975. Certain régimes, with a different political structure and social philosophy, have found it possible to raise rates of savings to 20 per cent or more in much shorter periods.

Within three years after the attainment of independence the government appointed a Planning Commission – a purely advisory body, even though Prime Minister Nehru has been its chairman from the outset – to develop a long-term strategy for economic growth. Development is a continuous process. The five-year plans have therefore been framed in the context of a long-term, continually evolving 'perspective plan'. The function of perspective planning is to relate economic development to social objectives and to provide a quantitative framework that expresses this relationship. It has to bring out the complex interdependence of the various sectors and to reveal possible obstacles to growth so that timely and coordinated action can be taken. Such an analysis is helpful in framing decisions regarding investments with long gestation periods, in the structuring of education in relation to the needs of society, in the reform of fiscal and financial institutions, and finally in the regional distribution of activity within the setting of national development.

Another function of the perspective plan is to educate public opinion on issues of development and to promote the kind of open discussion that is likely to secure a common consensus of political parties. This is perhaps easier in a poor society in which all can agree without controversy on at least one objective: the abolition of poverty. When the purpose is nothing less than to transform society, planning ceases to be an esoteric subject or a mathematical exercise. It must be imbued with deep social purpose and revolutionary

172

zeal. The problems must be boldly faced and alternatives must be discussed in concrete and quantitative terms, for the understanding, appreciation, and acceptance of the people.

In the course of time national political parties, instead of being labelled by ideology, may begin to be identified with the rates of growth they represent. The conservatives in India may then be those who urge a 5 per cent rate; the radicals, those who advocate a 7 per cent rate; and the men of reason and moderation, those who work for 6 per cent!

The basic strategy thus laid down for the five-year plans can be briefly outlined. Agriculture plays a dominant role in the Indian economy and is the sector that contributes principally to the supply of food and clothing that accounts for two thirds of the total consumption expenditure of the average Indian household. Much greater production of a variety of crops will be required. This will be possible only by enlisting advanced agricultural techniques: optimum utilization of water by irrigation and drainage, the use of organic and inorganic fertilizers, pesticides, better implements, more careful crop planning in relation to soil and climate, improved genetic strains, and reduction of crop losses by greater attention to storage and processing industries. The farmer has to have access to more knowledge and the requisite supplies, and he should have adequate incentive. Ultimately it is on the will, initiative, and effort of the millions of farmers that the outcome depends. As a palliative to widespread under-employment and low income in rural areas, particularly among landless agricultural workers, large programmes of labour-intensive rural works – forestation, road building, and land improvement through irrigation, drainage, and terracing – are being organized and carried out.

The role of industrialization in the scheme of things is not only to create new opportunities for employment but also to provide the technology and the fruits of technology that will improve the productivity and material condition of the people in the villages as well as in the towns. The economy of India is large and the potential size of the market is enormous. Even in the near future there is a great variety of products for which demand will be sufficient to allow production on an efficient scale in a few plants.

At this stage of its development India cannot produce all the things its growing economy requires. Although the industrial countries – and even some underdeveloped countries – have large exportable surpluses to pay for their imports, India – in common with most underdeveloped countries – labours under an export-import deficit (see 'The Structure of Development', by Wassily Leontief, page 129). This is partly because of difficulties in generating larger surpluses for export and partly because of tariff barriers erected by the industrialized countries. Since the creation of new industries and the increased requirements for intermediate materials generated by expanding industries give rise to large imports, the strategy of rapid development calls for heavy current foreign-exchange deficits in order to forestall endless, unmanageable deficits later on.

India has been receiving foreign assistance of about $1,000 million a year from a number of countries, including the U.S.S.R.; nearly 40 per cent has been contributed by the United States. If the momentum of development is to be maintained, foreign aid must continue to fill a gap of at least this order of magnitude in India's foreign-payments account for another decade.

The country must exert its utmost to expand its exports and at the same time India's friends must be prepared to accept and encourage such effort. Because of the continuing foreign-exchange shortage, India is compelled to continue restricting the entry of non-essential imports and regulating the availability of foreign exchange. This also means that the domestic development programme must aim at meeting most of the requirements of intermediate and finished manufactured goods. Concurrently India has to find ways to expand

and improve education, health, sanitation, and housing and to create social conditions for vigorous cultural advance. Coordinated development in all these fields is scarcely less important than expanding the supply of consumers' goods.

The urgency and complexity of the task, together with the possibility of achieving in this century substantial rapid gains by the harnessing of well-demonstrated technology, explain India's reliance on planning. In this still developing art the planner learns to project the pattern of the growth of 'final' demand arising from current consumption and investment and from the expenditures of government. The goods and services required by the 'indirect' demand of the productive sectors are also taken into account. Coupled with the consideration of saving on imports and of promoting exports, this is enough to give a good idea of the things to be produced. It turns out that fast development of industry is required, particularly in the metallurgical, fuel, machinery, and chemical fields. After careful consultation with state governments, the ministries of the central government and representative organizations and groups of the private sector, the targets of production are set. The state is directly responsible for providing the transport, power, major and medium irrigation, and the training and research facilities needed to sustain the agricultural and industrial expansion. Certain key branches of industry that are of a strategic nature or that involve large but slow-yielding investments are also developed under the auspices of the public sector. This leaves a large and expanding field for the private sector to explore profitably.

The development of agriculture and that of industry act and react on each other; they are complementary and not competitive. Their requirements are different and the scarce inputs they need are largely dissimilar. In agriculture and rural development the problem is primarily organizational. The organizational task of persuading 70 million households to function efficiently may well be the more difficult one, but it will not be rendered easier by curtailing the development of heavy industry.

Taken as a whole, the accomplishments during the first and second five-year plans have been considerable. The national income has risen from 99,000 million rupees ($21,000 million) in 1950–51 to 142,000 million rupees ($30,000 million) in 1960–61, in constant prices of 1960–61. In spite of an unexpectedly large population increase (totalling 80 million) during the decade, income per person has risen by 19 per cent. Agricultural output increased by 37 per cent and that of industry by about 100 per cent. Industrial growth brought significant diversification and consolidation, particularly in the basic metals, chemicals, fuel, and machinery industries.

In education, health, and other services the achievement has been heartening. In 1961 nearly 34 million children in the age group of six to eleven, some 60 per cent of the total in this group, were attending schools, compared with 19 million, or 43 per cent, in 1951. The number of students in higher secondary schools and universities has increased nearly two and a half times. The expansion in technical education is even more striking. By 1960 there were one hundred engineering and technical colleges in India compared with forty-nine a decade earlier. The enrolment in engineering colleges and in institutions teaching agriculture and veterinary sciences has increased fourfold since 1950, and the number of engineers per million population has increased from 150 to 250.

Significant progress in the control of mass communicable diseases such as malaria, smallpox, and cholera has brought a sharp reduction in the death rate. The life expectancy of the average Indian at birth is estimated to have increased by ten years – from thirty-two in 1950 to forty-two in 1960. A beginning has been made in establishing a nationwide system of health services; the number of hospitals and dispensaries has increased by nearly 50 per cent, and the number of hospital beds by one third. A central feature of the country's public health programme is the promotion of family planning, a topic on which the Indian people have evinced an altogether rational and receptive attitude.

A new dynamism, which can be sensed throughout the society, strengthens India's capacity for continued development. Valuable experience has been gained in the construction and operation of large and complex undertakings. The rate of investment, on which the future so largely depends, has been stepped up from 5 per cent to 11 per cent; the absolute volume of investment has nearly tripled during the past decade. Industrial investment in the five years of the first plan was less than 4,000 million rupees; it increased to 16,000 million rupees during the second plan, the share of the private sector rising from 3,400 million rupees to 8,500 million rupees. With the rapid expansion of domestic production of basic metals, chemicals, and machinery the the country has strengthened its capacity for accelerated development based increasingly on its own resource. In agriculture, the enlargement of irrigation potential, the establishment of the National Extension Services and the Community Development Programme (which now reaches more than half of the village population), the reconstitution of the village panchayats as organs of local self-government, and the extension of co-operative credit constitute the major forward steps.

In the third five-year plan (1961–6), now under way, the principal objective is to secure a rise in national income by 30 per cent, the pattern of investment being designed to sustain this rate of growth in subsequent periods. Agricultural production is to be increased by 27 per cent and developed in order to achieve self-sufficiency in food grains and substantial increases of other commodities to meet the requirements of industry and of exports to earn foreign exchange. In the industrial sectors the third plan and the perspective looking beyond it aim to secure sufficient increases in domestic production of steel, fuel, power, fertilizers and chemicals, machinery and equipment. An increase of industrial production by 70 per cent is envisioned, and the total investment of 104,000 million rupees will be somewhat in excess of the aggregate investment during the preceding ten years.

A fifth of this investment must be financed out of foreign aid. This fifth is critically important as a counterbalance to the deficit in foreign exchange and as a source of technical assistance, not merely as a supplement to domestic savings. Many countries of the world, regardless of ideology, have committed themselves to assisting India to make its plan a success.

Last year, just as the mobilization for development had begun to strain the resources of the nation, a military danger of unprecedented character arose on the northern frontier. In response to the invasion from China, defence had to be given an overriding priority; a massive rise in taxation, aggregating 20 per cent, had to be put through to meet its costs. The diversion of effort has upset frugally calculated plans; manufacturing capacities cannot be fully utilized; important work in scientific research is impeded for want of small amounts of foreign exchange; and the price level has shown a disturbing tendency to rise.

Nevertheless, the goals of the third five-year plan are being vigorously pursued. The achievement of these goals is vital to the success of the fourth five-year plan, projected for completion in 1970–71. By that time the country is expected to be in possession of capacity for annual production of 19 million tons of ingot steel, 250,000 tons of aluminium, 25 million tons of cement, about $4,000 million worth of machinery (including transport equipment), 170 million tons of coal, 24 million kilowatts of electric power, 2 million tons of nitrogenous fertilizers (in terms of nitrogen), 125 million tons of food grains, and 400 million tons of long-distance freight carried by railroads. Put alongside the figures for corresponding items in 1950 – steel ingots 1.4 million tons, aluminium 3,700 tons, cement 2.7 million tons, coal 33 million tons, electricity 2.3 million kilowatts of installed capacity, fertilizers 9,000 tons of nitrogen, food grains 50 million tons, and long-distance freight carried by railroads 92 million tons – it is easy to show the very large growth over twenty years. Elevated to these levels of output, the economy will have substantially increased its capacity for capital formation and self-sustained growth.

The long-term targets projected in the third plan are modest in relation to the needs of the people. Even with the plan fully realized, per capita income in 1975 will still be no more than $110, which is a third of the Japanese per capita income now. This factor underscores the urgency of accelerating the pace of development. There are uncertain elements in the picture. Agriculture is one of them; it is not too easy to see how to make it respond fully to treatment. Foreign exchange availability is another.

Will foreign aid be available at the right time – particularly in the present decade – and in the required magnitude? Can India hope to get the cooperation of friendly countries that will enable it to expand its exports? Will it be possible to think in terms of long-term commitments for aid and trade so that the long-range strategy India has in mind can be carried through successfully? These are questions to which India alone cannot give an answer. They are obviously important. Without foreign aid India will still continue to build its economy. However, it will be an uphill task, and progress will be slow. With assurance of aid India will not relax its efforts and indeed may find it possible to increase them.

The next decade is the crucial period. The strength and stability of this the most populous democracy in the world and the feasibility of economic and social transformation within the democratic framework are on test. Those of us who share a conviction in the humane values of an open society may hope that India's efforts will evoke the necessary understanding and material support from the international community.

The Development of Brazil

Although Brazil must still be classified as an underdeveloped nation, it is the most advanced of the nations in the Tropical Zone and is well on its way towards self-sustaining growth.

Brazil is undoubtedly the least known of the world's big countries. To most non-Brazilians it comes as news that Brazil stands fifth in geographic extent, eighth in population, and eleventh in gross domestic product. Still more significant is the news that Brazil has begun its industrial revolution. During the past twenty-five years the country's essentially rural economy, specializing in the production of a few tropical agricultural commodities for export, has been transformed into a recognizable industrial economy, with nearly half the population concentrated in urban areas. In this brief period, it appears, Brazilian industry has attained enough size and a sufficient degree of internal diversification to set the nation on the course of self-sustained economic growth.

On the basis of annual income per capita Brazil must still be classified as an underdeveloped country. In 1962 this figure was equivalent to about $380, as measured in cruzeiros with an internal purchasing power comparable to that of the U.S. dollar at home. The figure is somewhat lower when one converts cruzeiros into dollars at the prevailing rate of exchange; it is about $186. But even the larger figure is only a seventh that of the United States and not much more than twice the average prevailing in other underdeveloped countries. Multiplied by a population of 77 million, however, $380 per annum generates an internal demand that is already supporting the country's industrial development. During the past fifteen years the distinguishing trend of the economy has been the progressive substitution of consumers' goods manufactured within the country for products previously imported from the industrially developed economies abroad. By 1960 consumers' goods had fallen to 6.4 per cent of the total value of Brazilian imports; consumer expenditure for imported durable goods amounted to only 0.1 per cent of consumer income, and the expenditure for imported non-durable goods to 0.5 per cent.

A similar trend has become evident during this period in the importation of producers' goods and equipment. Although Brazil in 1961 depended on external sources for significant portions of its demand for basic materials – steel, aluminium, and heavy industrial chemicals and, to a greater degree, newsprint, fertilizer, and fuels – the expenditure for imported materials absorbed less than 2 per cent of aggregate current investment in that year. Brazil's own industrial system meets about 70 per cent of the country's demand for industrial equipment, particularly for heavy electrical machinery, machine tools, and oil-country gear. The principal role of imports in the economy has become the transmission of the more advanced technology available in North America and Europe.

That Brazil now verges on self-sustained development is evidenced by the fact that internal economic activity no longer depends on the volume of the country's exports and the prices they bring in the world market. Even in the recent period of decline in exports and commodity prices, the demand of the internal market has attracted investments at a rate adequate to maintain the growth of the economy.

To rank Brazil in the list of nations according to per capita income is to conceal at once the substantial development already achieved and the poverty and backwardness that remain to be cured. In the verdant and strongly industrialized savanna and plateau country of the south, Brazil is, on the annual-income-per-capita basis, very nearly a '$1,000 nation', to use the vivid terminology of

The map shows Brazil with labels including VENEZUELA, GUIANAS, COLOMBIA, RIO BRANCO, AMAPA, MANAUS, AMAZON, BELEM, AMAZONAS, PARA, MARANHAO, FORTALEZA, RIO GRANDE DO NORTE, CEARA, NATAL, PIAUI, PARAIBA, PERNAMBUCO, RECIFE, ACRE, RONDONIA, PERU, BOLIVIA, ALAGOAS, SERGIPE, GOIAS, BAHIA, SALVADOR, BRASILIA, MATO GROSSO, GOIANIA, MINAS GERAIS, BELO HORIZONTE, ESPIRITO SANTO, PARAGUAY, SAO PAULO, SANTOS, RIO DE JANEIRO, PARANA, CURITIBA, ARGENTINA, SANTA CATARINA, RIO GRANDE DO SUL, PORTO ALEGRE, URUGUAY, 0—400 MILES. Inset map: NORDESTE, AMAZON BASIN, CENTRAL PLATEAU, HUMID SEABOARD STRIP, PAMPAS.

BRAZIL is the fifth largest country in the world; its size in relation to South America is shown by the inset map at left centre. Although it is politically divided into twenty states, economic planners generally partition Brazil into five climatic and topographic regions, also shown on the inset and on the large map.

P. M. S. Blackett, the British physicist and student of economic development. On the range and in the dry-farming country of its drought-afflicted north-eastern interior, however, Brazil is still not far from being a '$100 nation'. The Amazon basin, which embraces fully half of the geographic domain but only 4 per cent of the population, presents still another stage of development, or lack of it: a great wilderness frontier awaiting a full assay of its resources, occupied here and there by some of the few remaining truly aboriginal peoples of the Western Hemisphere. It is not only the great size of Brazil that explains these disparities but also the vagaries of the history of the country since it came under European conquest and occupation more than four hundred years ago.

The land of Brazil was the first in the New World to yield an agricultural commodity for export to the Old. At a time when only the mining of precious metals brought adventurers and settlers across the Atlantic, the Portuguese established sugar plantations on the hot and humid seaboard of the continent south of the Amazon delta. The sugar production of the islands of the Atlantic – the Cape Verdes and the Madeiras – had already established a market in Europe and had given the Portuguese a head start in the arts of tropical agriculture. A century before the settlement of New England by the English the Brazilian plantations were on the way to achieving a monopoly over sugar as a commodity in international trade and as the principal agricultural commodity carried on the high seas. For two centuries the sugar industry – occupying the narrow strip of suitable land that reaches no more than 60 miles inshore and runs from the present state of Rio Grande do Norte southward 1,500 miles to the state of Paraná – provided the economic base for the occupation of Brazil. This economy rested from the outset on the labour of slaves imported mainly from Africa.

A few score of miles inland from the ocean a sharp climatic change reduces the annual rainfall to less than 20 inches and the rocky soil quickly loses the rain that falls. This is the Brazilian Nordeste (North-east), currently the country's most depressed region. The settlement of the Nordeste during the sixteenth and seventeenth centuries was occasioned mainly by the raising of cattle to supply draft beasts for the sugar plantations and mills. As time passed the region also entered world trade with the production and export of leather. The slave labour for this industry was recruited largely from the native Indian population.

To the New World, Portugal exported its feudal institutions. The land was deeded by the crown under *donatarios* to noblemen or others ennobled for the occasion; this gentry brought foremen, herdsmen, artisans, and labourers from the home country, but without women. The consequent intermingling of Portuguese with Indian and Negro blood has left its ethnic impression on modern Brazil: nearly half of the population is mestizo or mulatto and the people know no colour line today.

In the seventeenth century, as a result of the annexation of Portugal to Spain (from 1580 to 1640) and the war between Spain and the Netherlands, the Brazilian sugar region came under the domination of the Dutch, who controlled the refining and marketing of sugar in Europe. After a quarter century, in 1654, the Dutch were at last expelled from Brazil. Having meanwhile mastered the technology of sugar production, they proceeded to establish a competing plantation system in the West Indies, thereby liquidating the Brazilian sugar monopoly. Brazil now entered a long period of economic decline that ended in the first decade of the eighteenth century with the discovery of gold in the plateau region.

Throughout the eighteenth century Brazilian economic history was dominated by the expansion of gold mining and also of diamond mining. Brazil became, in fact, the main source of gold for the European economy during the period of fast development that culminated in the industrial revolution in England and, later, on the continent of Europe. The territory of the present states of Minas Gerais, Rio de Janeiro, and São Paulo were settled at this time by Europeans whose numbers began to offset the preponderance of African stock along the coast to the north.

The production of gold and diamonds declined in the last decades of the eighteenth century with the onset of the ultimate contest between England and France, signalled in North America by the French and Indian War and the American Revolution and followed in Europe by the French

Revolution and the Napoleonic Wars. The economic life of Brazil entered on a new course. The European settlements of the states of the south-central region, particularly in São Paulo, proceeded to develop a classical colonial export agriculture. Their position was consolidated in the middle of the nineteenth century, when coffee became a major commodity in international trade. During the last quarter of the century the coffee economy attracted a new flow of emigration from Europe to Brazil and made São Paulo the most densely populated region of the country.

The arrival of the automobile in the first decades of the present century brought the rain forests of the Amazon region into temporary prominence in the world economy. Brazilian plantations of the rubber tree *Hevea brasiliensis* were ruined by blight, however, and soon lost their markets to blight-free cultivation of the tree in the East Indies. The coffee economy of the country meanwhile also began to show symptoms of crisis. Successive periods of surplus production brought government intervention aimed at stabilizing the price by large-scale stockpiling. These oscillations reached their climax in the 1930s, when the Brazilian government, under the strong-handed administration of Getúlio Vargas, adopted the policy of deliberate destruction of coffee surpluses.

Thus throughout the four centuries from 1530 to 1930 the Brazilian economy depended on external demand to provide the stimulus for its growth. Three long-period cycles left their mark on the country's development: first, the impulse from sugar exports from 1530 to 1650; second, the dynamic impetus of gold from 1700 to 1780; third, the expansion of the world market for coffee from 1840 to 1930. The intervening periods of relative economic stagnation were marked by important political events. During the first of these periods, from 1650 to 1700, there began the great move for territorial expansion that carried the Brazilian borders far beyond the limits of the Treaty of Tordesillas, arranged by the Pope in 1493, which divided the world beyond the seas between Portugal and Spain. The second period, between 1780 and 1840, ushered in the independence of Brazil as a sovereign nation. Brazil became the seat of the Portuguese empire in 1807, when Dom João VI fled the Napoleonic conquest to set up his capital first in Bahia and then in Rio de Janeiro. His son Dom Pedro, whom he appointed regent on his return to Lisbon in 1821, became entrained in the movement towards independence and was proclaimed emperor of Brazil on 1 December, 1822. During the long reign of Dom Pedro II, who was installed as regent in 1831 at the age of five, was crowned emperor in 1840, and was forced into abdication and exile in 1889, the absolutist heritage of the Portuguese monarchy gave way to parliamentary institutions. Brazil became a constitutional republic in 1891, with a constitution modelled closely on that of the United States and a federal government strong enough to keep its vast territory united in a single state.

The discontinuities of this chronicle of development hold the explanation of the present extreme disparities of material existence in the country's various regions. Until very recent times development has gone forward in one region and then another without relation to conditions in the other regions or to the life of the nation as a whole. In regions and periods gripped by stagnation or decline, the people managed to survive by developing one or another kind of local subsistence economy without any self-sustaining impulse for growth. Where growth occurred it was based on the exploitation of resources in response to external demand.

This period in the economic history of Brazil came to an end in the world-wide economic crisis of 1929. The collapse of export-commodity prices cut the nation's import-purchasing power abruptly in half. Throughout the long depression of the 1930s the power of the federal government expanded as the coffee planters became increasingly dependent on the protections it could provide. The coffee plant is a perennial, and its yield cannot be turned on and off from season to season in response to the market. In order to avoid disaster in this sector the Brazilian government maintained the price to the coffeegrower by buying the unmarketable coffee – and burning it. Over the ten-year period 80 million bags of coffee were burned.

At current prices the coffee thus destroyed would amount to $3,200 million, or about a third of the net investment made in the country during the coffee-burning period. The government's action therefore had the effect of a daring compensatory (or 'deficit financing') policy; it maintained domestic purchasing power and facilitated the transition of the Brazilian economy towards freedom from its historic dependence on external demand. Although the policy also generated serious inflationary pressures, the maintenance of internal demand brought the Brazilian economy into the world market on favourable terms as an importer in view of the depression of prices, particularly the prices of used machinery and secondhand equipment. There began, therefore, a new phase in the development of Brazil, a phase based on internal demand. It was in this period that the trend towards the replacement of imports of consumers' goods by goods of local manufacture first asserted itself.

Investment funds formerly channelled to the production of coffee and other export products now flowed to the manufacturing of goods that had traditionally been imported. These investments not only amplified consumer purchasing power and hence the demand for such goods but also curtailed the supply of these goods from abroad by diverting available import funds to the purchase of intermediate materials and capital equipment used in manufacturing. The substitution of domestically manufactured goods for imported goods thus tended to be self-regenerating. There was no slackening of imports, because the new industries exerted such a strong demand for intermediate materials and capital equipment.

Demand in these sectors of the import trade has continued to grow ever since. This has weighted the balance of trade and of payments against the Brazilian economy, which is only too well known for its tendency towards external indebtedness. From necessarily slow beginnings in the coffee-burning period, however, the tempo of development has been stepped up until the present. The rate of increase in the gross national product averaged 5.8 per cent over the period from 1947 to 1961. Even after discount for the high rate of population growth this has yielded a net improvement of 3 per cent a year in income per capita. During the most recent five-year period the rate of increase in the gross domestic product has averaged 7 per cent – a figure compounded of a 4.8 per cent increase in agricultural production and a most impressive 12.7 per cent increase in industrial output.

Since the production of consumers' goods has been increasing at a rate identical with that of the gross domestic product, the driving impulse for growth must necessarily have been supplied by the rapid expansion of the capital-goods industries. The 1955-61 figures for these industries support the inference: a 100 per cent increase in steel production (to 2.5 million ingot tons); a 125 per cent increase in the output of the machine-building industries; a 380 per cent increase in electrical and communication equipment; and a 600 per cent increase in transport equipment.

The 4.6 per cent increase in agricultural production maintained over the past fifteen years is a creditable figure, and it has mounted to 4.8 per cent in the past five years. Nonetheless the gain has been largely offset by the growth of the population and still more by urbanization and the attendant increase in demand for a marketable surplus. Relatively speaking, the supply of agricultural goods has become smaller. Agricultural prices have consequently risen about 50 per cent faster than industrial prices in the course of the persistent inflation that has attended economic growth.

Bearing in mind that the process of substituting consumers'

goods produced at home for imported goods had been largely completed by 1957, the continued growth of the industrial sectors of the country is evidence of fundamental change in the structure of the economy as a whole. A typical agricultural economy is plainly undergoing transformation into an urbanized industrial economy. The decline in the ratio of foreign trade to gross national product is one of the key indices. It is a measure of Brazil's increasing independence of its former semi-colonial economic ties. The outlays for intermediate materials and fuels now make up the bulk of the import bill. They have been increasing each year, however, at a rate almost equal to that of the gross domestic product. These outlays constitute a measure of the advance still required to make the country's growth self-sustaining.

There is no doubt that Brazil's vast territory holds resources ample for its future development, even though these resources still remain largely uncatalogued. The scanty knowledge of these resources is in itself, of course, a symptom of underdevelopment. From what is known, however, it is clear that available technology – largely developed in regions of temperate climate and for the combination of resources found in the Northern Hemisphere – is by no means readily adaptable to the Brazilian tropics and to the country's peculiar assortment of resources. The immense forests of the Amazon basin, for example, await development by a technology that is still only incipient; Brazil meanwhile imports more than 20 per cent of its wood pulp and 70 per cent of its newsprint requirements. Similarly, extensive acreages of soil with good physical characteristics and adequate water lie idle for lack of an agricultural technique appropriate to them. Particularly cruel is the situation in the poverty-ridden Nordeste, where some 6 million acres of such soils go uncultivated.

Preliminary surveys show that more than 100 million acres of potentially arable land – twice the acreage now farmed – lie open to future exploitation. Of these lands only a fraction will require irrigation. To this abundance of land must be ascribed the fact that agricultural development in Brazil is still predominantly extensive, that is, by outward movement of the agricultural frontier. Of the 57 per cent increase in output achieved in the past decade, more than four fifths must be attributed to an increase in the area under cultivation and less than one fifth to the improvement in yield per acre, which, as Nevin S. Scrimshaw demonstrates in 'Food' (page 55), is the true frontier of agriculture.

Surveys of Brazilian mineral resources, still far from complete, indicate the country's immense industrial potential. Iron ores already prospected amount to more than 10,000 million tons and those inferred come to nearly 10,000 million more, altogether constituting two thirds of Latin-American reserves and 20 per cent of the world's known deposits. Reserves indicated by geology but still unsurveyed may be larger still. Known deposits of manganese total 60 million tons of high grade ore, and nearly 200 million tons of bauxite have been prospected. Nickel and tin are relatively abundant, but copper, lead, and zinc appear to be less so.

The principal obstacle to the exploitation of Brazil's huge iron resources is the lack of coking coal. This is an accident of geological history common to the underdeveloped nations of the Southern Hemisphere and serves as the prime example of the need for the development of an indigenous technology. In this case it is the need for a technique to accomplish the primary reduction of the ores by means other than the blast furnace, so well adapted to the concurrent abundance of coal and iron in the Northern Hemisphere.

Also in common with other Southern Hemisphere countries Brazil has comparatively thin energy resources. Coal reserves are estimated at about 2,000 million tons, a not very impressive figure by North American standards, and the coal is low in quality. The first substantial oil deposits have only recently been drilled; although proved reserves are expanding rapidly, they amount to a mere six-year supply at the present rate of consumption. Water power promises to yield no more than 30 million kilowatts, of which less than 5 million has been developed. Until technology brings in economically sound alternatives, Brazil must remain an importer of fuels.

Although the market economy has furnished the chief impetus to industrialization so far, it is becoming clear that maintenance of the present rate of growth will require increasing initiative in the public sector. Through the work of a central agency under the office of the President coordinating a system of decentralized planning, Brazil now has a three-year plan and the federal government is setting priorities in investment policy. The removal of the seat of the government to the nation's new capital in the frontier town of Brasília has played more than a symbolic role in directing the energies of the nation inward to the wealth of its interior.

Inevitably development has heightened the tensions between the emerging nation and the social institutions and power system that persist from feudal times. As recently as three decades ago the big landowners were the ruling class of Brazil. The abolition of slavery in 1888 gave way to a labour system characterized by deep social differences between employers and employed. Although the government was representative in form, it was almost exclusively operated from the top down; the executive power was able to select its own candidates in the legislative branch and enforce election results.

In 1930 there began a rapid dismantling of the old feudal agrarian system. With the decline of export agriculture, industrial entrepreneurs and the labour unions took a stronger hand in politics. Their growing power is inhibited, however, by the over-representation of rural areas in the electoral system and by an electoral law that disenfranchises the nonliterate majority of urban workers.

At present Brazil is a nation in transition. Its system of representative democracy has shown great flexibility in recent years, but this flexibility is now stretched to its limits. The most serious threat to peaceful transition arises from the fact that the most urgently needed reform – the political reform that will make the government more truly representative of the new urban and industrial society – has proved to be the most difficult to achieve. Until this higher degree of effective democracy is won, other institutional changes compelled by economic developments must generate dangerous tensions. The extension of social security to rural labourers, for example, has been pushed through only recently, after ten years of hard struggle in the federal legislature. The agrarian reform now being debated in the Brazilian congress will undoubtedly constitute a decisive test of the limits of pressure bearable by the present political system.

Brazil's approach to industrial maturity has great significance for the world as a whole, in view of the nation's extraordinary potentialities for future growth. By the end of the decade the population of Brazil will have come close to 100 million, with more than 60 million living in urban regions. Steel production will have exceeded 10 million tons and the foundations for self-sustained growth will have been secured. Because Brazil will be the first nation in the Tropical Zone to achieve industrialization, its culture and technology will surely have possibilities for worldwide projection. The democratic bias of the country's ethnic make-up will facilitate the projection of Brazilian values and ideals far beyond its own frontiers. Brazil is therefore bound to play an important role in relation to the new nations that are being formed in the tropical world.

The Development of the
U.S. South

ARTHUR GOLDSCHMIDT

Not so long ago the thirteen Southern states were an underdeveloped 'country' within the United States. An account of the process by which a quasi-colonial region was integrated into the national economy.

Just twenty-five years ago President Roosevelt released with his own endorsement a report by the National Emergency Council that described a region of the world whose 'potentialities have been neglected and ... opportunities unrealized'. The report told a story of inadequate housing, education, and health facilities, of an agriculture characterized by absentee ownership, single-crop farming, underemployment, and per capita incomes under $200 a year. Too poor to accumulate savings, the people had not developed their own industries and lived in a quasi-colonial economy, exporting staple crops and raw materials and importing most of the manufactured products they consumed.

The report dealt not with a region of Asia or Africa or Latin America but with the thirteen Southern states of the United States. In 1938 the U.S. South was an underdeveloped area within the most developed country in the world, 'the nation's economic problem No. 1'. Now, twenty-five years later, the South is emerging from that state of underdevelopment. It has attained the diversification of agriculture and industry and the potential for self-sustaining growth that characterize a viable modern economy. Although it still lags behind the rest of the United States, it has essentially achieved the economic goals towards which such countries as Nigeria, India, and Brazil are striving. These past twenty-five years of its hundred-year struggle with poverty illustrate the crucial importance of outside assistance to a people attempting to break through the interrelated barriers that bar the way to development.

These barriers, as the economist H. W. Singer has said, are a series of 'vicious circles within vicious circles and of interlocking vicious circles':

Poor people have poor health and low energy; low energy results in low productivity, which keeps people poor.

Absentee and large-scale ownership patterns demand single-crop farming, which is dependent on unstable markets, which dictate credit systems that perpetuate undesirable land-tenure patterns.

Economic development requires capital; capital must come from savings; saving requires cutting down consumption – but a poor economy must consume most of what it produces.

Low economic activity cannot create the tax base for producing the revenue required for such 'infrastructure' investments as transport, power, and education – which are essential to increased economic activity.

Development activity in poor areas is initially more effective in reducing death rates than in producing goods; consequently populations increase and living levels are lowered.

Development requires change, but in the traditional societies of underdeveloped regions power is often in the hands of those most bound by tradition and resistant to change.

The Swedish economist Gunnar Myrdal has described these vicious circles as a downward-spiralling 'cumulative process of circular causation'. It can be summed up by the saying 'Poverty is its own cause'. These deterrents to development affect pockets of poverty within the developing, and even the most developed, nations as well as the underdeveloped countries of the world. It is true that technology and industry offer the means of distributing wealth and well-being throughout a country, and that today the more highly developed a society becomes, the more it tends to achieve economic equality for its people – a modern version of the egalitarianism of primitive hunting-and-gathering societies. The process, however, does not spread automatically from one sector or section to others. Rather, unevenness of development is implicit in the process of development. Disparities of income, differences in the state of technology and consequent productivity, and wide variations in levels of living are the conditions of any society that has left the moorings of its primitive economy and launched on the turbulent process of development.

The principal disparity within the developing countries is a sharp discontinuity between the economies of the agricultural mass of the country and the capital city or a few main industrial centres. But sometimes whole areas have stood still or retrogressed in an otherwise developing economy, either because they are 'new' areas, remote from the original focal points of development (the old U.S. West, Siberia, western China, and western Australia), or because they are physically inhospitable regions (eastern Bolivia and eastern Peru). Others are bypassed for more complex economic and political reasons and fail to share in the economic development of the rest of the country. While these regions lag they are a serious brake on the progress of the whole economy. The depressed Nordeste of Brazil is one such bypassed area in a developing country. In a more advanced country, Italy, the southern provinces have yet to share fully in the benefits of a modern economy.

The U.S. South was similarly bypassed in the course of the nation's industrial development. It was not just that the South's cotton-tobacco-slave economy cut it off from the commercial and industrial advance of the rest of the nation or that it suffered directly from the Civil War and Reconstruction. According to classical economics the operation of the market and the play of trade should tend to equalize development between the advanced and the retarded parts of a country. Myrdal has pointed out that the process is not

THE U.S. SOUTH, as discussed in this chapter, comprises the eleven Confederate states plus Kentucky and Oklahoma. Its area, 863,000 square miles, is almost twice that of the six-nation European Common Market; its population, 48,802,000 in 1960, is 27

that simple. If there are 'spread effects' that move outward to elevate the poorer regions, there are also 'back-setting effects': patterns of trade, migration, and the movement of

per cent of the population of the nation. Most of the South,
stretching all the way from tidewater Virginia to the cattle ranges
of Texas, has a long growing season and adequate rainfall.

capital within a country favour the rich and developing
sections at the expense of the poor and underdeveloped sections. Myrdal suggested that national policy can intervene

to strengthen the spread effects, and that this is what has happened in most of the advanced nations. But in the case of the United States, Federal intervention tended historically to aid the development of the North and to retard the South.

U.S. Government intervention in development reached back to the Articles of Confederation; indeed, concern with national development was the proximate cause of the meeting of state delegates at Annapolis in 1786 that called the Constitutional Convention. Homesteading policies, beginning with the Northwest Territories Ordinance of 1787, coupled with the disposition of large grants of public lands for infrastructure investment in transportation and education, were intentionally designed to promote development and to spread it westward across the continent. These Federal policies had little applicability in the South, where there were no extensive public lands left for disposal. Tariff policies designed to help the industrialized sections of the country did so at the expense of the raw-material-producing Southern states. The University of Texas historian Walter Prescott Webb, in his 1937 book *Divided We Stand*, struck out at what he called the 'economic imperial control of the North', attacking not only Government policies of discrimination but also policies of corporations that affected Southern development: restrictive licensing arrangements, discriminatory pricing systems, and investment of insurance funds in Northern industry. He showed that even the Civil War pensions (predominantly paid to Northerners) were related to the tariff policies of the Federal Government because these payments, which provided purchasing power for Northern business, were a convenient method of siphoning off the embarrassment of riches that the U.S. Treasury reaped from tariff revenues. Webb's complaints were reminiscent of those of the 'New South' movement in the 1880s and of the Populists in the 1890s. But the nation as a whole had largely ignored these pleas. The South remained in a stagnant backwater outside the mainstream of U.S. development.

In June 1938, President Roosevelt called attention to the need for national involvement in the South's efforts at development. At his request the *Report on Economic Conditions of the South* mentioned at the beginning of this chapter was drafted by a group of Southerners in the Federal service and reviewed by an advisory committee of Southern citizens. The report did not have any formal status, nor was it in any sense a 'plan' for the South. Written in simple language and high dudgeon, it was an effort to gain support for reversing policies of drift and discrimination and putting the influence of the Federal Government behind the development of the South. Its impact was felt throughout the country.

In examining 'the factors that have produced the present economic unbalance' between the South and the rest of the country, the report covered to a remarkable extent the same range of problems discussed by experts currently reviewing similar underdeveloped segments of the world for the United Nations, the World Bank, or U.S. foreign-aid agencies.

The paradox of the South is that while blessed by immense wealth, its people as a whole are the poorest in the country. Lacking industries of its own, the South has been forced to trade the richness of its soil, its minerals and forests, and the labour of its people for goods manufactured elsewhere.

This might describe the majority of the countries of Asia, Africa, and Latin America.

'The farming South depends on cotton and tobacco for two thirds of its cash income,' the report continued. 'More than half of its farmers depend on cotton alone.' With the characteristic insularity of its day the report stated that 'no other similar area in the world gambles its welfare and the destinies of so many people on a single crop market year after year', ignoring the rice farmers of Thailand, the tea gardeners of Ceylon, the coffee-growers of Colombia.

More than half of the South's farmers were tenants, and tenancy dictated one-crop farming, because 'landlord and tenant usually have not been able to find a workable method of financing, producing, and sharing the return from such crops as garden truck, pigs, and dairy products'. One-crop farming in turn made soil conservation practices almost impossible – as it still does in many parts of the world. Inefficient use and control of water resources retarded economic development. Malaria afflicted more than two million Southerners, and the low-income belt of the South was 'a belt of sickness, misery, and unnecessary death'. In the slums of 'overcrowded, economically undeveloped Southern communities' lived families that shuttled 'from farm to mill or mine and back again to farm', always with 'too little income to enable their members to accumulate the property that tends to keep people stable'. For years many had been 'living only half-employed or quarter-employed or scarcely employed at all'.

The South comprised 28 per cent of the U.S. population but its banks held less than 11 per cent of the nation's bank deposits and less than 6 per cent of the savings deposits. Because money was scarce interest rates were high, making borrowing difficult for industry, for local governments, and in particular for farmers, who had to pay interest as high as 20 per cent (as do borrowers in the less-developed countries today). The South had to 'look beyond its boundaries for the financing of virtually all of its large industries and many of its small ones'. Outside financing turned policy-making power over to 'outside management', a circumstance that disturbs many of the emerging countries now seeking capital from abroad.

The report insisted that the South was short-changed in its terms of trade with the rest of the country, and it hammered away at the Government policies it considered responsible. Unwarranted differentials in railroad freight rates made it more expensive to ship manufactured goods to centres of consumption in the North and the Middle West from the South and from equidistant factories in the Northeast. High tariffs helped Northern industry but made it difficult for foreign countries to acquire dollars with which to buy Southern raw materials. The South was caught in a vice that has kept it from moving along with the mainstream of American economic life. On the one hand, the freight rates have hampered its industry; on the other hand, our high tariff has subsidized industry in other sections of the country at the expense of the South.

Low incomes and revenues kept the infrastructure of Government services meagre. 'Since the South's people live so close to the poverty line, its many political subdivisions have had great difficulty in providing the schools and other public services necessary in any civilized community.' In 1936 the state and local governments of the South collected in taxes only $28.88 per person compared with $51.54 in the nation as a whole. 'The South must educate one third of the nation's children with one sixth of the nation's school revenues.' Not only were there inadequate schools and colleges but there were also 'meagre facilities . . . for research that might lead to the development of new industries especially adapted to the South's resources.' The lack of opportunity in the South was causing large-scale migration; 'many of its ablest people' were leaving, just as is the case today in so many of the less-developed countries.

Adding up all these factors in terms of individual incomes, the report found that in 1937 the average annual income of Southerners was $314 compared with $604 for other Americans. In none of the Southern states did the per capita income reach the national figure; in more than half of the states incomes were below 60 per cent of the U.S. average; in three they were less than half. Industrial wages were about two thirds of those paid elsewhere in the United States. For the farmers it was worse: even in 1929 Southern farm families had a per capita gross income of $186. For the tenant farmers it was still worse: the average cotton tenant family's income was $73 per person and share-croppers' earnings ranged down to $38 per person. These figures are within the range of incomes in most poor countries of the world today.

The South was in 1938 a kind of colony of the United

States, but it was a built-in colony. The traditional antidote to colonialism – independence – was not appropriate. Only economic integration with the nation as a whole could cure the South and close the North-South gap. And this integration could be accomplished only by Federal action. There is a direct parallel today in the economic development of the former colonial regions of the world. Independence, although it is a political and moral imperative, does not in itself bring economic development. The emerging nations need to be integrated into the structure of the developed world's economy. No amount of bootstrap-pulling can do the job; outside assistance is essential.

The report made few specific recommendations for the amelioration of the conditions it found, but it did call implicitly for action by the Federal Government: greater Federal expenditures for public works, resource development, and relief; more favourable credit facilities, particularly for agriculture; correction of discriminatory freight-rate and tariff policies. The tone was occasionally xenophobic, but there was no demand for economic 'independence'; the message was national, emphasizing the interdependence of Southern development and U.S. economic health. 'The South is the nation's greatest untapped market. . . . Northern producers and distributors are losing profits and Northern workers are losing work because the South cannot afford to buy their goods.' In spite of the complaints against freight-rate discrimination and tariffs, the report called not for a return to *laissez faire* but for the 'national integration policies' and the 'state interferences' that Myrdal says are required to keep a region or sector from lagging far behind in the development of a national economy.

Twenty-five years after the publication of the report the nation's major preoccupation with the South is no longer economic. To be sure, the income patterns of the Southern states still put all of them below the line of the national average, but the trend throughout the intervening years has been towards closing the gaps: the lower-income states have moved upward towards the national level while that level itself has moved upward. There are still geographic disparities in employment and income in the United States, but the contrast is now largely between scattered depressed enclaves (many of them still in the South) and the rest of the country. Economists generally agree that this integration of the U.S. economy was brought about not by the unseen hand of economic forces but by the long arm of national policy.

It is doubtful that the principal direct proposals of the report – the removal of the freight-rate differentials, the relaxing of restrictions on the sale of margarine or even the lowering of tariffs – had any substantial role in effecting the rise of the economy of the South. Nor were the relief payments called for enough to provide more than a temporary palliative. The conditions reported in 1938 were not caused by the depression but merely highlighted by it, and they required changes more drastic than countercyclical measures of employment and relief. Even Federal grants-in-aid to the Southern states, which had lagged on a per capita basis and were stepped up in 1939, did not rise appreciably above the national average until ten years later.

The measures that achieved the most spectacular changes were those that attacked the root problems of Southern agriculture: 'land reform' (in the broad sense used by the U.N.), including not only changes in land tenure but also improvements in farm credit, marketing, research, and other services. These changes were effected in the South through Federal measures designed to correct the tenure and technology of agriculture and to increase its productivity. Programmes of supervised rural credit and other aids to the lowest income farmers, as well as broader programmes of research, soil conservation, and price supports, have radically changed the patterns of Southern agriculture.

The small, uneconomic farms are disappearing. There are more than one million fewer farms under 50 acres in the South than there were in 1935. The total number of farms has dropped from 3,263,000 to 1,572,000 and the average acreage per farm has doubled. Most impressive of all is the fact that there are some 1,400,000 fewer tenant farms today than there were in 1935. Tenants operate less than a fourth of the farms, compared with more than half in 1935. There were more tenant families in 1935 than there are farms today in the South.

Farm practices, too, have undergone basic changes. Soil and moisture programmes have changed the very landscape of the South. Where once there were gullied hillsides and worn-out soil there is now a rich farmland improved by contour ploughing, run-off-retardation works on small streams, supplementary irrigation and reforestation. In 1959 a third of the number of cotton farms with 60 per cent of the acreage produced a bigger cotton crop than in 1939. Although the South still produces most of the cotton of the United States, the appalling dependence on that commodity has been ended. In part this has been the result of a technological change, the mechanization of cotton farming, that resulted in increased cotton production in Texas and Oklahoma and on irrigated farms in the arid South-west, forcing the South-east to diversify its crops. Roads and rural electrification have added appreciably to the productivity of Southern agriculture. The South received more than 41 per cent of the total loans of the Rural Electrification Administration from its inception, in 1935, to 1961.

The agrarian reform of the South is not yet complete. The problem of tenancy has been replaced to some extent by the problem of the farm wageworker. Sixty-five per cent of the full-time farm labourers receive less than $5 a day in wages, and their average total annual income in 1960 was less than $800. But the net income per Southern farm had risen by 1960 to 87 per cent of the national average. More important than this relative rise was the absolute rise: at $6,238 in 1959 the gross money income per farm was nearly eight times the 1939 figure.

The agricultural sector was not the only front on which the Government moved to alleviate the conditions cited in the report. Water-conservation and development projects, led by the pace-making Tennessee Valley Authority programme, brought navigation channels, flood-control benefits, and power to the region. The TVA power policies, in the American tradition of eschewing monopoly and spreading widely the benefits of public resources, affected rates and service far beyond its own network of transmission lines. Federal projects on the Red, the White, the Arkansas, the Savannah, and the other major rivers of the region developed hydro-electric power that was firmed and augmented by the South's vast natural gas, oil, and coal resources, so that the region now has nearly 30 per cent of the nation's generating capacity. The South's consumption of electric power increased from 21 per cent of the nation's production twenty-five years ago to more than 30 per cent in 1960.

Industrial development was directed to the South by the Defense Plant Corporation and other World War II agencies. But the new manufacturing plants of the South have been attracted also by more basic considerations, notably the ready availability of natural resources. The South produces more than 63 per cent of the country's crude oil and 78 per cent of the natural gas, and the expanding demand for petrochemicals has made a manufacturing industry out of what was once an extractive industry only. The South's new wealth in hydro-electric power has brought in chemical and metallurgical industries – notably aluminium – that require large amounts of electricity. These and the increased number of pulp and paper mills are among the growing resource-based industries that have joined textiles and tobacco. Meanwhile enlarged markets have attracted decentralized rubber and automobile assembly plants. By 1955 manufacturing had replaced agriculture as the leading source of personal income in the South. Whereas in 1929 agriculture had supplied about 26 per cent of the South's 'earned' personal income, in 1961 it provided less than 9 per cent; in the same period manufacturing's share rose from 16 per cent to 22 per cent.

Gross weekly earnings of production workers in the South were still below the U.S. average of $92.34 in 1961. Earnings in Texas topped this average by a few cents, but at the other end of the scale workers in Mississippi averaged $61.93. These figures, however, are affected by the types of industry in the region; in any given industry the wages paid in the South and in other parts of the country tend to be closer. Hourly earnings of textile production workers averaged $1.57 in New England in 1958, compared with $1.45 in the South-east; the spread was even narrower in fine cotton goods, with New England's average $1.56 and the South-east's $1.52. Federal minimum-wage legislation and the spread of union organization helped to integrate the South in the national economy. As a result the South was receiving 20 per cent of the nation's total personal income in 1955, compared with only 16 per cent in 1929. The per capita personal income in the South was 76 per cent of the national figure in 1961; in 1929 it had been only 57 per cent.

Southern housing is still below the national level. The 1960 census of housing reveals that the percentage of housing units classed as 'dilapidated' is twice as large in the South as in the rest of the country. But the actual number of such units is only 1.5 million, whereas the 1938 report concluded that 4 million families in the South needed to be rehoused. In the twenty-five years, Federal programmes to stimulate home-building and help people to buy homes had brought housing in the South closer to the national standard.

Rising incomes have made it possible for the Southern states to invest more in education; their spending per pupil rose from half of the U.S. figure in 1936 to more than 70 per cent in 1959–60. The Southern states, however, are still far down on the scale: Mississippi spends only 55 per cent of the national figure, South Carolina 56 per cent, Arkansas 60 per cent. Even to attain these low school-spending levels the Southern states must devote a higher proportion of their citizens' incomes to education than the rest of the nation does. This is not only because of generally low income but also because of an unfavourable age distribution (more children), a larger proportion of children in public schools (fewer Catholics), and the added expense of maintaining lingering segregated school systems. As a result the South ranks high on a 'sacrifice' scale relating spending on education to personal income. With the United States at 100, such a scale shows Mississippi at 125, South Carolina at 115, and Arkansas at 110.

Population control is often advocated to mitigate the problem of low incomes. In the South this has to some extent been accomplished by migration, both within and out of the Southern states, which has appreciably redistributed their population. (High birth rates have kept the total population at about the same proportion of the national total, even though people have been leaving most of the states.) From 1940 to 1960 the South (excluding Florida) had a net loss of 5.6 million people through out-migration. Together with movements within the region this has resulted in a sharp relative increase in the number of people living in Florida and Texas and a relative decline in most of the other states, with absolute decreases in population in Mississippi, Oklahoma, and Arkansas.

Economic progress in the South has been spotty and the development process is not yet complete, but this underdeveloped section of the United States has come a long way. Many of the vicious circles of self-enforcing poverty have been broken – and with them many of the traditional relations and patterns of living that may well have held the South back but have also been basic to its sense of its own identity, to a regionalism that could never be completely explained by geography, economics, or even history. Development inevitably brings social upheaval and political tensions. As in the case of so many developing countries, some of the concomitants of economic change are deeply disturbing to many Southerners. In this situation fear of the future and nostalgia for the past occasionally outweigh courage and eagerness for progress. But the forces of Southern development and the nation's need for that development will not be denied.

The distinguished Southern historian C. Vann Woodward has suggested in his *Burden of Southern History* that the South's perspective on history is closer to the world's view than is that of the rest of the country because the South has shared with nearly all the peoples of Europe and Asia the experiences of military defeat, occupation and reconstruction. The South has shared another tremendous experience with the developing countries of the world: it has within recent years faced their problem of breaking the vicious circles that thwart development. It is an irony of history that this section of the United States, which presents to the world such a disturbing picture of human relations because of the turbulent current effects of its development, should offer to the emerging countries so important a message bearing on their own concerns. Economic development is too important to leave to the blind play of economic forces; it can be hastened or hindered by the intervention of policies designed to increase productivity and promote welfare. And the process is strengthened by outside assistance. The rich nations of the world will have to do for the poor nations what the Federal Government of the United States did for the South.

The Planning of Development

EDWARD S. MASON

Future development will not strictly parallel classical industrial revolutions. Technology, economics, and ideology all make it likely that governments will play a central role in directing the process.

The side-by-side existence in the modern world of developed countries and underdeveloped countries has suggested to generous and hopeful citizens of both kinds of country that the poverty of the latter can be cured by the rapid, systematic, and large-scale transfer of the technology that has produced such great wealth for the former. Development is not, however, a matter of technology alone. The underdeveloped world cannot, in the words of one observer, 'simply import the industrial revolution from abroad, uncrate it like a piece of machinery, and set it in motion'. The availability of modern industrial technology is a fact of great importance; it should assure that developing countries will not need to experience all the difficulties encountered by the Western countries in their achievement of self-sustaining growth. But putting this technology to effective use requires something more than borrowing it.

The borrowing, in the first place, involves the recipient country in economic and political as well as cultural relations with the lending country. At their present stage of development most developing countries are heavily dependent on the flow of foreign capital. Their creditors cannot realistically expect, however, that they will follow the precedents of development in the past to some predetermined and agreed-on destination. As the more extensive reviews of the status and progress of Nigeria, India, and Brazil in the preceding pages have shown, the developing nations have entered on their present course from diverse historical backgrounds and a variety of economic situations. They include some of the world's oldest nations and some of the newest; some of the largest nations in domain and population and some of the smallest. Some are faced with heavy overpopulation, some with underpopulation, and all with high rates of population growth; the differences among them in the ratio of population to resources are great. One group of underdeveloped countries, particularly the oil-rich countries, has readily exploitable and exportable resources to finance development; many others have difficulty scraping together an agricultural surplus for export. The prospects for development among the underdeveloped countries are as disparate as the conditions from which they have started.

In general it can be said of these countries that they are predominantly free-enterprise economies. Yet in all of them, without exception, governments are attempting to play a role in the development process substantially larger than the one Western governments played at corresponding stages in the development of their countries. There appear to be few underdeveloped countries without a four-year, five-year, or six-year development plan. Yet in most of these countries there is little discernible relation between the announced purposes of the plan and what in fact gets done. Plainly the various objective and ideological considerations that condition the approach to development among the underdeveloped countries deserve the careful and sympathetic understanding of the citizens of nations that preceded them in the technological revolution.

Economic development requires a set of institutions, habits, incentives, and motivations such that the inputs necessary to a continuous increase in output are self-generating. The essential inputs are capital, trained manpower, and technology, and they are likely to be self-generating only in an environment in which the population seeks to improve its physical well-being and in which the rewards of effort are at least roughly proportional to the productivity of effort.

There are some countries – Burma may be an example – in which material improvement does not rank high in the scale of values accepted by most of the population. It is difficult to see under such circumstances how the inputs necessary to increased outputs are to be generated. There are other countries in which the reward for effort is siphoned off into other hands by landholding and land-use arrangements or by corrupt and rapacious governments. In Iran, at least prior to the current land reform, the share of the crop accruing to the cultivator was too low to induce increased effort. It would be well to recognize that in various parts of the underdeveloped world the prospects for economic growth will not become particularly bright until there are some rather profound changes in human motivations and values and in the socio-political structure. It is a mistake to think that economic development enjoys a high priority throughout the underdeveloped world. Some populations and in particular some ruling groups definitely prefer the status quo.

Nevertheless, in most of the countries under consideration here, national income has been growing somewhat faster than population, in spite of an acceleration in the rate of population growth, and in some countries it has been growing a good deal faster. Brazil, Greece, Israel, and Taiwan seem to have attained what can be called a self-sustaining and satisfactory rate of economic development. India, Pakistan, the United Arab Republic, Turkey, the Philippines, Colombia, and perhaps a few other countries appear to have fair prospects of reaching this goal within the next decade or two. In these countries savings as a proportion of national income are increasing, education and training programmes are producing results, and the spread and adaptation of Western technology, assisted in some cases by extensive foreign aid, is stimulating productivity. Nigeria and the other new nations of Africa south of the Sahara have much longer roads to travel.

The appropriateness of the dominant role in development asserted by their government is rarely questioned by public opinion in underdeveloped countries. Indeed, the pressure of opinion is usually in the direction of accelerating and expanding public action deemed necessary to the achievement of a rapid rate of growth. Whether or not the policies followed by these governments are those most conducive to development is a different question. At present, however, what they do or fail to do has relatively little effect on the day-to-day material condition of the people.

In countries with per capita incomes of less than $100 a year the share of government in national income customarily runs from 6 or 7 per cent to about 15 per cent. Where per capita incomes range upward to $700, as in some Latin-American countries, the government's share runs somewhat above 15 per cent. In western Europe and the United States the figure varies between 20 and 30 per cent. There is thus a rough correlation between per capita incomes and the share of government in national product.

In non-Communist countries around the world, it would seem, the poorer the country, the larger the role of private enterprise in its economic life. This generalization requires closer examination. The reason for the preponderance of the private sector in developing economies is not far to seek. They are overwhelmingly agricultural economies, and this is true also of developing countries, such as China, that have Communist governments. Indeed, it can be reasonably assumed that in any country in which income per capita is under $100 a year, 50 to 70 per cent of its labour force will be employed in agriculture.

Such industry as exists will be predominantly handicrafts. Trade is almost exclusively in the hands of small merchants. Agriculture, handicrafts, trade, and services are traditionally private activities and in underdeveloped countries must be expected to account for 80 per cent or more of total employment and around three quarters of total income.

From this one might conclude that what is done to stimulate activity in the private sector will generate more economic development than anything done in the public sector.

The dominance of the private sector at this juncture in the life of low-income countries obscures the role their governments seek or are called on to play in their development. If one looks at the figures for new investment, that role becomes clearer. In Latin-American countries from 40

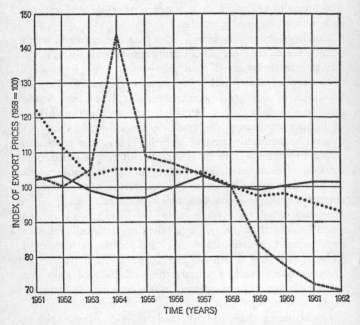

TERMS OF TRADE have been unfavourable for the underdeveloped nations. The prices of their exports have gone down (*dotted line*), while those of the developed countries' exports, which they must buy, have been stable (*black line*). Fluctuating commodity prices are a particular problem. The broken line traces the price index of a commodity group consisting of cocoa, tea, and coffee, which are key exports respectively of Nigeria, India, and Brazil.

to 50 per cent of new investment is typically public. In India well over 50 per cent of planned investment is in the public sector. In Pakistan the figure is closer to two thirds. Nor is the role of government in the channelling of economic activity limited to the area of public investment as conventionally defined. Functions that typically belong to the sphere of private enterprise in developed countries are frequently confined to the public sector in developing countries. The exploitation of mineral resources and the development of basic industries such as steel, fertilizer, and cement are common examples.

Furthermore, in those activities that are confined to the private sector the flow of economic resources is by no means left to the direction of market forces. The geographical dispersion of new private investment is controlled by the provision of overhead-capital facilities in certain regions and their denial in others. Problems created by the shortage of foreign exchange are typically met by rationing the quantities available among various claimants; such allocation of foreign exchange is a powerful device in directing the flow of private resources. Frequently it is supplemented by licensing, price controls, the regulation of new security issues, and other measures. Even in Puerto Rico, which probably relies on private – largely foreign – investment more heavily than almost any other underdeveloped area, development is stimulated and guided by government. Indeed, the government of Puerto Rico often builds and finances plants and, through the activities of an enterprising planning agency, ferrets out economic opportunities for private business.

Government, then, in most underdeveloped countries attempts to do much more in promoting economic development than it is customary for governments in advanced countries to do, and much more than it is usually supposed governments did in Western countries at similar stages of their development. It is appropriate to ask why this is so and if government in many low-income countries is not, in fact, attempting to do too much. No flat judgement can be rendered here, In the first place, the impression that governments left development to private enterprise during the 'classical' phase of the industrial revolution is at least partly an illusion. In England, it is true, the government on the whole limited itself to providing the proper atmosphere and left the rest – including even road building, port development, and education – to private enterprise. This was not true elsewhere, however; certainly not in the United States, where government furnished the infrastructure and, as in the case of the railroads, provided substantial subsidies from the public domain for private enterprise.

Perhaps the foremost example of government-stimulated and government-guided development in any private-enterprise economy is provided by Japan. Here the state directed investment by establishing publicly owned enterprises, undertaking joint ventures with private capital, subsidizing private investment and guaranteeing returns, and buying extensively for its own military and civilian accounts. In the decade after 1870 the state built and operated such diverse enterprises as mines for coal, copper, and gold; iron foundries; shipyards; machine shops; model factories for cement, paper, glass, sulphuric acid, cotton spinning, and many others. Undoubtedly the government's most fruitful contribution to the expansion of social capital was in the realm of education. The Japanese government seems, in fact, to have adapted its educational expenditures specifically to development purposes.

The emphasis given in much of the underdeveloped world to government-promoted development is not, therefore, without precedent. Nevertheless, it remains true that these governments are taking a stronger hand in development than the governments of the now developed private-enterprise countries did at corresponding stages in their history. In part this is the result of objective circumstances that condition the current development process; in part it is no doubt the product of an ideology that differs substantially from the one dominant in the early nineteenth century.

Foremost among the 'objective' considerations is the large priority that must be given to roads, railways, harbours, power generation and distribution, communications, irrigation, industrial estates, and the like. In most developing countries the capital requirements for such facilities will account for something like 50 per cent of the total investment. Although private capital used to be available for some of these purposes – foreign private capital, for example, financed railroad construction, telephone and telegraph systems, and electric utilities at an early stage in Latin-American development – this is no longer the case. Indeed, existing privately owned facilities have been and are being acquired by Latin-American governments at a rapid rate. In sum, the investment role thrust on government in developing economies is likely to be a big one.

Government participation in the transfer of technology is also likely to be large. The early development of industrial technology in the West was undertaken by skilled artisans and tinkerers working in the eighteenth-century equivalent of the twentieth-century garage, and the exploitation of new techniques went forward in the hands of individual and family firms operating in an environment relatively free from government control. Now that these techniques have been developed, however, they can be borrowed. In the borrowing process government enterprise is not as inappropriate as it probably would be in early stages of technical development. The modern application of these techniques requires large-scale units, the financing of which lies outside the capability of family-sized firms or the pools of private capital domestically available in underdeveloped countries. The transfer of technology through government agencies may well be inevitable. Here again the Japanese example suggests that in the early stages of industrialization large-scale intervention by government can facilitate and accelerate the process.

During the nineteenth century foreign private investment and enterprise were the overwhelmingly important agencies of technical transfer in most underdeveloped areas. It is still important, and dollar for dollar it is probably the most efficient form of transfer. But foreign private investment finds few opportunities in certain areas, and for various reasons it is unwelcome in others. It is now extensively supplemented by the technical-assistance programmes of governments and the technical agencies of the United Nations. Currently these programmes involve expenditures of at least $500 million a year. This type of technical transfer inevitably involves the extensive participation of government in the aid-receiving country.

Much the same sort of thing has been happening in the area of capital transfer. During the nineteenth century private investment accounted for all but a small fraction of the flow of capital into underdeveloped regions. Although some of these funds went to finance publicly owned utilities, the amounts, as a proportion of total foreign investment, were small. In 1961, on the other hand, of the total flow of $8,750 million in long-term funds from developed to underdeveloped countries outside the Soviet bloc, nearly $6,000 million represented public loans and grants. (Aid from the Soviet bloc to developing countries outside comes to substantially less than $1,000 million, mostly in the form of long-term loans at low interest rates and payable in commodities.) Most of these funds were used to finance activities in the public sector. This tendency is reinforced by the fact that the international and national lending and granting agencies perfer large projects; large projects in countries without highly developed private enterprise fall in the public sector. Whereas a loan or grant to cover the foreign-exchange requirements of a development programme can and does find its way into the private sector, project lending for large installations stacks the cards against private enterprise of the sort that flourishes in most underdeveloped countries.

Certain aspects of this massive flow of funds deserve closer examination. In the first place, the $8,750 million does not include military assistance. Since the settlement of the Algerian question almost all the funds under this heading have come from the United States and have been running at an annual rate of $1,500 million to $2,000 million. As is well known, these outlays tend to be concentrated in the seven or eight countries on the perimeter of Asia. Military expenditures, of course, compete with economic-development expenditures as claimants for available resources, both in the developing countries and in the U.S. aid programme. What is not so obvious is that expenditures for these presumably divergent purposes are to a certain extent complementary. Military roads and bridges are usually available for civilian use. In a number of developing countries the army is an effective agency for promoting literacy and the teaching of useful skills. Although military expenditures are likely to handicap economic development, a certain degree of complementarity should be recognized.

Of the $6,000 million in long-term public funds provided by the West to the developing countries in 1961, approximately 90 per cent took the form of bilateral aid. Most of the remainder came through U.N. agencies, principally the International Bank for Reconstruction and Development and the International Development Association. To an increasing extent, however, bilateral aid is coming under some form of multilateral coordination. Consortiums composed of various countries and agencies are now formed to finance the development programmes in India, Pakistan, Turkey, and certain other countries. Consultative groups of various countries belonging to the Development Advisory Committee with headquarters in Paris are beginning to coordinate bilateral aid to a number of developing countries. The countries of the European Common Market now coordinate aid to associated overseas areas.

The United States in 1961 provided roughly 60 per cent of the public funds made available to underdeveloped countries by the West. This includes the shipment of agricultural surpluses under Public Law 480, passed by Congress in 1954. Valued at world-market prices, surplus-food shipments have been running to about $1,500 million a year. For certain countries this type of aid is as good as gold. In the United Arab Republic, for example, where land adapted to wheat cultivation is strictly limited, scarce foreign exchange otherwise available for development would, in the absence of these food shipments, have to be used for food imports. In other countries, however, the availability of U.S. food surpluses on a grant basis may lead to a rate of importation seriously damaging to domestic agricultural development. Agricultural surpluses are of substantial assistance in economic development and their volume is likely to increase rather than decrease, but these shipments cannot be equated dollar for dollar with other types of economic assistance.

The total flow of long-term funds, public and private, is of critical importance to the developing world at the present stage. Whether or not this flow is likely to increase it is difficult to say. Foreign private investment could undoubtedly be stimulated in a number of developing countries by a more receptive attitude. A diminution in the pace of the armament race would in all probability increase the flow of public funds. Under present circumstances, however, foreign aid can hardly be described as a politically popular undertaking in any advanced country.

Meanwhile, it must be admitted, the past decade's decline in the prices of the export commodities that earn foreign exchange for the underdeveloped countries has substantially discounted the aid they have received. In cocoa, tea, and coffee – crucial exports of Nigeria, India, and Brazil – the index shows an average decline of more than 30 per cent.

The objective considerations that tend to bring governments into such a prominent role in development are reinforced by less tangible considerations of ideology. In the first place, many of the élite now occupying important government positions in underdeveloped countries were trained in the West during the period when nineteenth-century capitalism, with its emphasis on the 'rights of property', was giving way to a 'welfare state' capitalism, egalitarian in character and more concerned with 'human rights'. In their view it is necessary as well as appropriate to use the power of the state to lessen inequalities in the distribution of income and to give protection to less privileged elements in the population.

Among the 'demonstration effects' of the West that impress an observer in many underdeveloped countries is the prevalence of the demand for social services of all sorts. According to one authority, 'most underdeveloped countries want the blessings of the welfare state today, complete with old-age pensions, unemployment insurance, family allowances, health insurance, 40-hour week, and all the trimmings.' In Western countries a sustained growth in national output antedated the spread of social services of this type. Throughout most of the currently underdeveloped world, demand for these services here and now is all but politically irresistible. This shift in political values obviously assigns to government functions that are new and frequently difficult to administer.

Although the weakness of the private sector in many underdeveloped countries helps to explain the ascendance of government in their economic life, the pressure in this direction is frequently accentuated by a latent hostility to private enterprise, particularly foreign private enterprise. Such hostility is seen in the exclusion of private enterprise from certain areas of economic activity, in the preferred position given to public enterprise when it comes to the allocation of scarce foreign exchange, and in the detailed and pervasive controls set up to assure that no private action conceivably harmful to the public interest, as understood by government officials, can take place. Perhaps it is not so much a question of hostility to private enterprise as of misplaced confidence in the ability of public administrators to direct in minute detail the proper course of economic activity.

Ideological predilections in many underdeveloped countries take the form of not very well defined types of local socialism. In India one hears of a 'socialist pattern of society'. In the United Arab Republic the merits of Arab socialism are extolled. In various newly emergent African countries people speak of 'African socialism'. Without attempting to specify the meaning of these varieties of socialism, it can be said that they tend to encourage and rationalize the initiative of government in the promotion of economic development.

In attempting to acquit the heavy responsibilities thus assumed or thrust on them, the governments of underdeveloped countries espouse planning as the preferred, if not essential, development technique. The record shows, however, that the espousal of planning, from country to country, is more eloquent than its execution. The plan as it emerges from the planning agency may fail to win acceptance as a programme of action by political authority; or, if the plan is ratified by duly constituted authority, political pressures and interministerial rivalries may cause development expenditures to depart from its prescriptions; or the resources and requirements as envisioned by the plan may turn out to be so remote from actual capabilities that the plan loses significance as a set of political directives.

Examples can be cited in support of all these observations. Indonesia has never, since its independence, been without a plan. But no plan has enjoyed sufficient political support to have had significant effect on the course of the economic development – or non-development – of that country. Various Latin-American countries have framed development plans but, in the absence of effective budgetary control over spending ministeries, large differences have opened up between the word and the act. The United Arab Republic, which has done better than most, operates under a development plan that calls for a doubling of national income in ten years. Since this target is considerably in excess of what Egyptian resources will permit, the actual growth rate falls short of the projected rate. The setting of overambitious targets, furthermore, has had a demonstrably adverse effect on the allocation of the country's domestic and foreign-exchange resources.

These examples do not constitute an argument against planning but against confusing the mere existence of a plan with effective planning. The assumption by government of anything like a directive role in the economy inevitably requires some sort of planning. The plan may be limited to the establishment of priorities in public investment and of some consistency in the policies affecting the private sector. Indeed, in this limited sense of planning, the United States, like Molière's prose-speaking Frenchman, has been planning throughout its national life. The underdeveloped countries go further than this. It seems clear that wherever government deliberately seeks to accelerate the rate of development, effective economic planning is an essential part of the process.

The planners' principal concerns are three: how to increase the amount and quality of resources available for economic development, how to allocate public investment among the various development projects in the public sector, and how to stimulate private production within the bounds established by the objectives of the development programme as a whole. With respect to the first of these concerns, the expansion of resources available for investment involves not only the limitation of consumption in favour of savings but also, over a period of time, the direction of investment into the most productive channels. Under private enterprise this is the traditional function of market incentives. In underdeveloped economies, where public investment is so large a part of the total, the establishment of investment priorities becomes perhaps the central task of planning.

Planning agencies are of course advisory to political decision-makers, and it goes without saying that planning will inevitably reflect the political characteristics of the government being advised. A totalitarian government may be able single-mindedly to pursue an objective at variance with the desires of a majority of the population. A democratic government could not follow such a course of action for long. Moreover, the structure of the government institutions, the class composition of the population, and the competition of special interests will inevitably affect the character of the plan. All of this does not mean that democratic planning must be an economically irrational compromise of divergent political pressures. But it does mean that economic calculations operate within a fairly severe set of limitations.

A single-minded concern with economic growth might dictate an exploitation of economic opportunities in the order of their prospective social rates of return, but political influences may urge a geographically 'equitable' dispersion of public investment. The economic calculus may indicate a thorough-going programme of land reform as one of the most promising steps towards economic development. But political realism intrudes to suggest a policy of the second best. Confronted with severely limited resources, the development planners may be compelled, as in Nigeria (see 'The Development of Nigeria', page 149), to pare down the allocation to social services and to primary education in favour of 'productive' investment and technical training.

The fact that political forces 'choose' objectives other than that of maximizing the rate of economic growth does not make these choices irrational. Even from the point of view of economic growth a geographical distribution of public funds dictated by political expedience may be desirable if such a distribution contributes to political stability. These are, moreover, national planning objectives apart from economic growth. The political process not only sets limits to economic calculation but also impinges on planning in more positive ways. A government strongly committed to economic development and enjoying the support of the governed can release and organize human effort that has not previously been put to effective use. Something like this was accomplished by the Japanese in the late nineteenth century, and something like it may be in process of accomplishment in present-day India.

In those democratic underdeveloped countries that have been making substantial economic progress, the major difficulties lie not in the interference of political interests with economic calculation nor in the quality of the economic analysis itself but rather in the fact that the administrative machinery has lagged behind development plans. A due regard for this limitation would hold down the size of the public investment programme to dimensions capable of effective management; it would counsel against the imposition of controls whose execution is outside the competence of existing public services; it would emphasize the importance of necessary changes in government procedure.

To recite the mistakes, difficulties, and limitations of the planning process in various developing countries is not to argue against planning as an essential technique of development. There are important objective reasons as well as ideological reasons why the role of government in planning and promoting economic development must be large.

The Authors

ASA BRIGGS ('Technology and Economic Development') is Dean of Social Studies, Professor of History, and Pro-Vice Chancellor at the University of Sussex. A native of Yorkshire, Briggs received an M.A. in History from the University of Cambridge with first class honours in 1941 and a B.Sc. in Economics with first class honours at the University of London. He was a Fellow of Worcester College, Oxford from 1945 to 1955 and Reader in Recent Social and Economic History. From 1955 to 1961 he was Professor of Modern History at Leeds University. Among his publications are *Victorian People* (1954), *The Age of Improvement* (1959), *Chartist Studies* (1959), *The Birth of Broadcasting* (1961), *Victorian Cities* (1964), and *The Golden Age of Wireless* (1965). He is President of the Workers' Educational Association and a member of the University Grants Committee.

KINGSLEY DAVIS ('Population') is professor of sociology and chairman of International Population and Urban Research at the University of California at Berkeley. He was graduated from the University of Texas in 1932 and acquired an M.A. and a Ph.D. from Harvard University in 1933 and 1936 respectively. After teaching for a year at Clark University he joined the faculty of Pennsylvania State College, where he was made head of the sociology department. In 1942 he went to Princeton University to work in the Office of Population Research; he was a member of the Princeton faculty until 1948, when he was appointed associate director and later director of the Bureau of Applied Social Research at Columbia University. From 1946 to 1952 he was a member of the joint committee on South Asia of the Social Science Research Council, and from 1952 to 1954 he directed a research project on population trends and demographic behaviour in Jamaica. He joined the Berkeley faculty in 1955. Davis served as U.S. representative to the United Nations Population Commission from 1955 to 1961.

NEVIN S. SCRIMSHAW ('Food') is professor of nutrition and head of the Department of Nutrition and Food Science at the Massachusetts Institute of Technology. A graduate of Ohio

Wesleyan University, Scrimshaw received an M.A. and a Ph.D. from Harvard University in 1939 and 1941 respectively. He did post-doctoral work in nutrition and endocrinology at the University of Rochester and received an M.D. from that university's medical school in 1945. After interning at Gorgas Hospital in the Canal Zone, he returned to the University of Rochester in 1946 to do research in the department of obstetrics and gynaecology. In 1948 he went back to Panama to do field research on nutrition and pregnancy and shortly thereafter became chief of the Nutrition Section of the World Health Organization's Pan American Sanitary Bureau. From 1949 to 1961 Scrimshaw served as director of the Institute of Nutrition of Central America and Panama. He acquired a degree in public health from Harvard in 1959 and was adjunct professor of public health nutrition at the Columbia University College of Physicians and Surgeons from 1959 until 1961, when he took up his present post. Scrimshaw has served as adviser on world nutrition problems to various Government and United Nations agencies. At M.I.T. he is currently engaged in studies involving the effect of stress on nutritional requirements and of nutrition on resistance to infection and on mental development.

ROGER REVELLE ('Water') is University Dean of Research at the University of California and director of that university's Scripps Institution of Oceanography. Revelle began his long association with the Scripps Institution in 1931, two years after acquiring an A.B. in geology from Pomona College. He received a Ph.D. from Scripps in 1936 and was professor of oceanography there in 1951, when he became the first alumnus of that institution to be appointed its director. During World War II Revelle served as a commander in the U.S. Navy and immediately after the war joined the Office of Naval Research as head of the Geophysics Branch. In 1946 he organized the oceanographic expedition associated with the atomic bomb test in Bikini Lagoon, measuring the diffusion of radio-active waters and their effects on marine organisms. During the early 1950s he led several other expeditions to the central and southern Pacific, developing new methods for measuring the flow of heat out through the floor of the ocean. He served as president of the first International Oceanographic Congress held by the United Nations in 1959, and in 1961 he became the first man to hold the post of science adviser to the Secretary of the Interior. Revelle is currently president of the Committee on Oceanographic Research of the International Council of Scientific Unions and a member of the U.S. Commission to the UNESCO Office of Oceanography.

SAM H. SCHURR ('Energy') is director of the Energy and Mineral Resources Programme of Resources for the Future, Inc., a private research organization sponsored by the Ford Foundation. Schurr acquired his B.A. and M.A. degrees from Rutgers University in 1938 and 1939 respectively and shortly afterwards joined the staff of the National Bureau of Economic Research. During World War II he served in the Office of Strategic Services and on the War Production Board. From 1946 to 1949 he did research on the economic aspects of atomic power for the Cowles Commission for Research in Economics at the University of Chicago. He was appointed chief of the manufacturing and mining branch of the U.S. Bureau of Labor Statistics in 1949 and a year later became chief economist for the U.S. Bureau of Mines. Schurr spent a year doing economic research for the Rand Corporation before taking up his present post in 1954.

JULIAN W. FEISS ('Minerals') is staff assistant for metals to the Assistant Secretary of the Interior for Minerals and Fuels. He is also assistant to the director of the U.S. Geological Survey. Feiss was graduated from Princeton University in 1927 with honours in geology and did graduate work at the Arizona School of Mines before going to Africa as field geologist with the Rhodesian Congo Border Concessions in 1929. He returned to this country three years later to become consulting engineer with the firm of Crowell and Murray. This work took him to mine sites in northern Canada, Chile, and Peru. In 1938 he became geologist at the Climax Molybdenum Company's mine in Climax, Colorado – the largest underground metal mine in the U.S. During World War II Feiss served in Kenya and Ethiopia as liaison officer to the King's African Rifles. After the war he was editor of *Mining Congress Journal* for two years before joining the U.S. Bureau of Mines in 1947. From 1952 to 1961 he worked as geologist for the Kennecott Copper Corporation.

FREDERICK HARBISON ('Education for Development') is professor of economics and director of the Industrial Relations

Section of Princeton University. He was graduated from Princeton in 1934 and acquired his Ph.D. there in 1940. During World War II he served as consultant to various Government agencies dealing with labour and manpower problems. In 1945 he went to the University of Chicago to become professor of economics and executive officer of that university's Industrial Relations Centre. He held both posts until 1955, when he joined the Princeton faculty. In 1962 Harbison was in Geneva as a member of a committee to explore methods of forecasting world manpower and education requirements for the International Labour Organization. He returned to Geneva early in 1963 as a delegate to the United Nations Conference on the Application of Science and Technology for the Benefit of the Less Developed Areas. Harbison is currently a member of the Special Commission on Education, Science and Culture of the Alliance for Progress and consultant to various Government and international organizations, including the National Planning Association, the U.S. Department of Labor, the Agency for International Development, the Organization for Economic Cooperation and Development, UNESCO, and the Peace Corps.

WASSILY LEONTIEF ('The Structure of Development') is Henry Lee Professor of Economics and director of the Economics Research Project at Harvard University. Born in St Petersburg, Russia, in 1905, Leontief was graduated from the University of Leningrad with the title of 'Learned Economist' in 1925. He did research in economics at the University of Kiel and at the University of Berlin, receiving his Ph.D. from the latter institution in 1928. In 1929 he went to Nanking as economic adviser to the Chinese government and two years later came to this country to do research at the National Bureau of Economic Research. He joined the Harvard faculty in 1931. During World War II Leontief served as consultant to the U.S. Department of Labor, where he applied his 'input-output' system of analysis to the problems created by the impending shift from a wartime to a peacetime economy. He has also served the United Nations as consultant on the economic aspects of disarmament and on the economic development of newly emerging countries.

WOLFGANG F. STOLPER ('The Development of Nigeria') is professor of economics at the University of Michigan. He is currently on leave from that university and is doing research at the Centre for International Affairs of Harvard University. Stolper was born in Vienna in 1912 and studied at the universities of Berlin, Bonn, and Zurich before coming to this country in 1934. He received an M.A. and a Ph.D. from Harvard in 1935 and 1938 respectively and afterwards taught at Harvard and at Swarthmore College before joining the Michigan faculty in 1949. Stolper first worked on problems of economic development in 1946 when he co-authored, with Chiang Hsieh, the report *Social Policy in South-east Asia* for the International Labour Office. On leave from Michigan during the academic year 1955–6, he did research at the Centre for International Studies at the Massachusetts Institute of Technology that resulted in a book, *The Structure of the East German Economy*. In 1960 he was appointed head of the Planning Unit of the Nigerian Ministry of Economic Development and spent most of the next two years in Lagos, working out Nigeria's first economic-development plan. Earlier this year Stolper was in Malta as chief of the United Nations Economic Mission to that country.

PITAMBAR PANT ('The Development of India') is Chief of the Perspective Planning Division of the Indian Planning Commission. A physicist turned economist, he received his master's degree from the University of Allahabad in 1939 and stayed on as lecturer in physics. Before long, however, he was jailed for his activities in the Indian independence movement. Upon his release after two and a half years, he returned to the movement as secretary to Jawaharlal Nehru and had a central role in the labours that brought about the independence of his country and the organization of its government in 1947. Pant then withdrew from politics to work with P. C. Mahalanobis, another physicist turned economist, who was the organizer and director of the Statistical Institute of Calcutta. Together they framed the basic philosophy of Indian economic planning. In 1952, Pant joined the Planning Commission in his present capacity. He is also Joint Secretary of the Indian Statistical Institute and was closely identified with the introduction of decimal coinage and the metric system into India. With his wide experience and his dedication to 'purposive and peaceful social and economic transformation', Pant is well known beyond the borders of India as an original contributor to the theory and practice of economic development and is in demand as a consultant to the governments of other new nations and to international agencies.

CELSO FURTADO ('The Development of Brazil') is head of the Superintendency for the Development of the North-east (SUDENE) and minister without portfolio in the Ministry of Planning Affairs of the João Goulart government. Furtado was born in the city of Pombal in the state of Paraíba in 1920 and was graduated from the National Faculty of Law of the University of Brazil at Rio de Janeiro. He received a Ph.D. in economics from the University of Paris in 1948 and did research for a year at the University of Cambridge before joining the permanent team of economists attached to the United Nations Economic Commission for Latin America in 1949. He later became chief of the Development Division of ECLA and worked on problems of economic development in Brazil, Mexico, and Venezuela. In recent years Furtado has served the Brazilian government as Minister for Economic Planning and Development and as Director of the National Bank for Economic Development.

ARTHUR GOLDSCHMIDT ('The Development of the U.S. South') is Director for Special Fund Activities in the United Nations Department of Economic and Social Affairs. Goldschmidt was born and raised in Texas and was graduated from Columbia University in 1932. A year later he joined the newly formed Federal Relief Administration and subsequently worked for various other Government agencies, including the Senate Committee on Interstate Commerce, the National Bituminous Coal Commission, the National Power Policy Committee, and the Department of the Interior. During this period he was one of a group of southerners in Government who prepared the 'Report on Economic Conditions in the South' discussed in the present article. In 1944 he was appointed director of the Division of Power in the Department of the Interior. He served on the National Commission for UNESCO in 1949 and was U.S. delegate to the U.N. Scientific Conference for the Conservation and Utilization of Resources. Goldschmidt joined the U.N. Secretariat in 1950 as a director in the Technical Assistance Administration and was appointed to his present post in 1959. His work has taken him to most of the developing countries of Asia, Africa, and Latin America. He wishes to make clear that the views expressed in this article are personal and not necessarily those of his institution.

EDWARD S. MASON ('The Planning of Development') is Lamont University Professor of Economics at Harvard University. A graduate of the University of Kansas, Mason received an M.A. from Harvard in 1920 and a B.Litt. from the University of Oxford in 1923. He returned to Harvard later in the same year to become instructor in economics, acquired his Ph.D. from that university in 1925, and has been a member of the Harvard faculty ever since. Over the past twenty-five years Mason has served as economic consultant to various Government agencies, including the Department of Labour, the Office of Strategic Services, and the State Department. In 1947 he was appointed chief U.S. economic adviser to the Moscow Conference of Foreign Ministers. From 1947 to 1958 he was dean of the Harvard Graduate School of Public Administration.

Bibliography

TECHNOLOGY AND ECONOMIC DEVELOPMENT

Gruber, Ruth, ed.: *Science and the New Nations: The Proceedings of the International Conference on Science in the Advancement of New States at Rehovoth, Israel.* Basic Books, Inc., 1961.

Higgins, Benjamin: *Economic Development: Principles, Problems, and Policies.* W. W. Norton & Company, Inc., 1959.

Hoselitz, Bert F.: *Sociological Aspects of Economic Growth.* The Free Press of Glencoe, 1960.

Lewis, W. Arthur: *The Theory of Economic Growth.* George Allen & Unwin Ltd, 1955.

Rostow, W. W.: *The Process of Economic Growth.* W. W. Norton & Company, Inc., 1952.

POPULATION

Banks, J. A.: *Prosperity and Parenthood: A Study of Family Planning Among the Victorian Middle Classes.* Routledge & Kegan Paul Ltd, 1954.

Coale, Ansley J., and Hoover, Edgar M.: *Population Growth and Economic Development in Low-Income Countries: A Case Study of India's Prospects.* Princeton University Press, 1958.

Davis, Kingsley, and Blake, Judith: 'Social Structure and Fertility: An Analytic Framework'. *Economic Development and Cultural Change*, Volume 4 (April 1956), No. 3, pp. 211–35.

Freedman, Ronald, Whelpton, Pascal K., Campbell, Arthur A.: *Family Planning, Sterility and Population Growth.* McGraw-Hill Book Co., Inc., 1959.

Population Control. Law and Contemporary Problems, Volume 25 (Summer 1960), No. 3, pp. 377–629.

Taeuber, Irene B.: *The Population of Japan.* Princeton University Press, 1958.

FOOD

Desrosier, Norman W.: *Attack on Starvation.* Avi Publishing Co., Inc., 1961.

Science, Technology, and Development, Volume III: Agriculture. United States Papers Prepared for the United Nations Conference on the Application of Science and Technology for the Benefit of the Less Developed Areas. U.S. Government Printing Office, 1962.

Science, Technology, and Development, Volume VI: Health and Nutrition. United States Papers Prepared for the United Nations Conference on the Application of Science and Technology for the Benefit of the Less Developed Areas. U.S. Government Printing Office, 1963.

WATER

Langbein, W. B., and Hoyt, W. G.: *Water Facts for the Nation's Future.* The Ronald Press Company, 1959.

Mass, Arthur, Hufschmidt, Arthur, Dorfman, Robert, and Thomas, Harold: *Design of Water Resources Systems.* Harvard University Press, 1962.

Possibilities of Increasing World Food Production: Basic Study No. 10. Food and Agriculture Organization of the U.N., 1963.

Revelle, Roger: 'Mission to the Indus'. *New Scientist,* Volume 17 (February 1963), No. 326, pp. 340–2.

Stamp, L. Dudley, ed.: *A History of Land Use in Arid Regions: Arid Zone Research, XVII.* UNESCO, 1961.

Water Resources: A Report to the Committee on Natural Resources. Publication 1000-B. National Academy of Sciences–National Research Council, 1962.

Woollman, Nathaniel: *The Value of Water in Alternative Uses.* University of New Mexico Press, 1962.

ENERGY

Civilian Nuclear Power: A Report to the President, 1962. U.S. Atomic Energy Commission, 1962.

Schurr, Sam H., Netschert, Bruce C., Eliasberg, Vera F., Lerner, Joseph, and Lansdberg, Hans H.: *Energy in the American Economy, 1850–1975: An Economic Study of Its History and Prospects.* Johns Hopkins Press, 1960.

Science, Technology, and Development, Volume I: Natural Resources – Energy, Water and River Basin Development. U.S. Papers Prepared for the United Nations Conference on the Application of Science and Technology for the Benefit of the Less Developed Areas. U.S. Government Printing Office, 1963.

Searl, Milton F.: *Fossil Fuels in the Future.* U.S. Atomic Energy Commission, 1960.

Bibliography

Zapp, A. D.: 'Future Petroleum Producing Capacity of the United States'. *U.S. Geological Survey Bulletin 1142-H*. U.S. Government Printing Office, 1962.

MINERALS

Bateman, Alan M., *Economic Mineral Deposits*. John Wiley & Sons, Inc., 1942.

Bibby, Geoffrey: *The Testimony of the Spade*. Alfred A. Knopf, Inc., 1956.

Steinman, David B., and Watson, Sara Ruth: *Bridges and Their Builders*. Dover Publications, Inc., 1941.

Street, Arthur, and Alexander, William: *Metals in the Service of Man*. Penguin Books, 1944.

Thirring, Hans: *Energy for Man: Windmills to Nuclear Power*. Indiana University Press, 1958.

EDUCATION FOR DEVELOPMENT

De Witt, Nicholas: *Education and Professional Employment in the U.S.S.R.* U.S. Government Printing Office, 1961.

Harbison, Frederick H., and Myers, Charles A.: *Education, Manpower and Economic Growth*. McGraw-Hill Book Co., Inc., 1964.

Kerr, Clark, Dunlop, John T., Harbison, Frederick, and Myers, Charles A.: *Industrialism and Industrial Man: The Problems of Labour and Management in Economic Growth*. Harvard University Press, 1960.

Orleans, Leo A.: *Professional Manpower and Education in Communist China*. National Science Foundation. U.S. Government Printing Office, 1960.

THE STRUCTURE OF DEVELOPMENT

Analyses and Projections of Economic Development, Number 6: The Industrial Development of Peru. U.N. Economic Commission for Latin America, 1959.

Barna, Tibor, ed.: *Structural Interdependence and Economic Development: Proceedings of an International Conference on Input-Output Techniques, Geneva, September, 1961*. St Martins Press, 1963.

Chenery, Hollis B., and Clark, Paul G.: *Interindustry Economics*. John Wiley & Sons, Inc., 1959.

Leontief, Wassily, and others: *Studies in the Structure of the American Economy: Theoretical and Empirical Explorations in Input-Output Analysis*. Oxford University Press, 1953.

THE DEVELOPMENT OF NIGERIA

Annual Abstract of Statistics. Federation of Nigeria. Federal Office of Statistics, 1960 and 1961.

Coleman, James S.: *Nigeria: Background to Nationalism.* University of California Press, 1960.

Economic Survey of Nigeria: 1959. National Economic Council of Nigeria, 1959.

Handbook of Commerce and Industry in Nigeria. The Federal Ministry of Information, 1962.

National Development Plan: 1962–68. Federation of Nigeria. The Federal Ministry of Economic Development, 1962.

THE DEVELOPMENT OF INDIA

India 1962. Ministry of Information and Broadcasting, 1962.

Malenbaum, Wilfred: *East and West in India's Development.* National Planning Association, 1959.

The New India: Progress through Democracy. Planning Commission, 1958.

Programmes of Industrial Development: 1956–1961. Planning Commission, 1958.

Second Five Year Plan. Planning Commission, 1956.

Third Five Year Plan: A Draft Outline. Planning Commission, 1960.

THE DEVELOPMENT OF BRAZIL

The Economic Development of Latin America in the Post-war Period. U.N. Economic Commission for Latin America, 1963.

Furtado, Celso: *The Economic Growth of Brazil: A Survey from Colonial to Modern Times.* University of California Press, 1963.

Los Recursos Naturales en América Latina, Su Conocimiento Atual y Investigaciones Necesarias en Este Campo. U.N. Economic Commission for Latin America, 1963.

Rosenstein-Rodan, P. N.: 'International Aid for Underdeveloped Countries'. *The Review of Economics and Statistics,* Volume 43 (May 1961), No. 2, pp. 107–38.

THE DEVELOPMENT OF THE U.S. SOUTH

Clark, Thomas D.: *The Emerging South.* Oxford University Press, 1961.

Hoover, Calvin B., and Ratchford, B. U.: *Economic Resources and Policies of the South.* The Macmillan Co., 1951.

Bibliography

Myrdal, Gunnar: *Rich Lands and Poor: The Road to World Prosperity.* Harper & Row, Publishers, 1958.

Webb, Walter Prescott: *Divided We Stand: The Crisis of a Frontierless Democracy.* 1937.

Youngson, A. J.: *Possibilities of Economic Progress.* Cambridge University Press, 1959.

THE PLANNING OF DEVELOPMENT

Heilbroner, Robert L.: *The Great Ascent.* Harper & Row, Publishers. 1963.

Hirschman, Albert O.: *The Strategy of Economic Development.* Yale University Press, 1960.

Mason, Edward S.: *Economic Planning in Underdeveloped Areas.* Fordham University Press, 1958.

Promoting Economic Development: The United States and Southern Asia. Claremont College, 1955.

Mead, Margaret, ed.: *Cultural Patterns and Technical Change.* New American Library, 1955.

Nurske, Ragnar: *Problems of Capital Formation in Underdeveloped Countries.* Oxford University Press, 1953.

MORE ABOUT PENGUINS
AND PELICANS

If you have enjoyed reading this book you may wish to know that *Penguin Book News* appears every month. It is an attractively illustrated magazine containing a complete list of books published by Penguins and still in print, together with details of the month's new books. A specimen copy will be sent free on request.

Penguin Book News is obtainable from most bookshops; but you may prefer to become a regular subscriber at 3s. for twelve issues. Just write to Dept. EP, Penguin Books Ltd, Harmondsworth, Middlesex, enclosing a cheque or postal order, and you will be put on the mailing list.

Two other books published by Penguins are described overleaf.

Note: *Penguin Book News* is not available
in the U.S.A.

TWO IMPORTANT NEW PENGUIN
REFERENCE BOOKS

THE PENGUIN ENGLISH DICTIONARY

Containing more than 45,000 entries and specially prepared for Penguins by a team led by Professor G. N.
Garmonsway of London University, this new dictionary
places particular emphasis on current usage. Definitions,
which include hundreds of post-war words and senses,
are as direct and simple as possible, and a new and
immediately understandable system is introduced as a
guide to pronunciation. In all *The Penguin English Dictionary* makes an unrivalled catalogue of English words
as used today in print and speech.

THE PENGUIN ENCYCLOPEDIA

This concise and authoritative new encyclopedia has
been geared deliberately for use in the second half of the
twentieth century. Articles by specialists, under more
than 6,000 main headings, pay particular attention to the
rapidly advancing areas of science and technology; but
the arts and humanities have not been neglected. These
simple, accurate, and intelligent explanations are likely
to prove equally handy for the schoolboy, the student,
and the family bookshelf. Specially commissioned for
Penguins, this up-to-date work is remarkably comprehensive and fully cross-referenced. It will be followed by a
gazetteer and a dictionary of biography.